WHEN DO I GET TO PLAY?

Holding God's hand through
extraordinary challenges.

Brian D. Watkins

WESTBOW
PRESS®
A DIVISION OF THOMAS NELSON
& ZONDERVAN

WestBow Press books may be ordered through booksellers or by contacting:

WestBow Press
A Division of Thomas Nelson & Zondervan
1663 Liberty Drive
Bloomington, IN 47403
www.westbowpress.com
844-714-3454

ISBN: 978-1-6642-1531-3 (sc)
ISBN: 978-1-6642-1532-0 (hc)
ISBN: 978-1-6642-1530-6 (e)

Library of Congress Control Number: 2020924186

Print information available on the last page.

WestBow Press rev. date: 03/08/2021

CONTENTS

For Donielle and all of the DREAMS families.

INTRODUCTION

"What I am doing, you do not understand
now, but you will understand later."

~ John 13:7

Years ago, I remembered having a conversation with my mother about
some ridiculous questions I would ask when I was a small boy. Questions
she didn't have the answer to, items that didn't have an answer at all.
I was only about four or five years old when my philosophical side
began to emerge with these deeply profound questions of the universe.
One of her favorites that I asked was, "Mom, how big would I have to
be so I could eat our house?" Her answer, of course, "Don't be silly,
you can't eat our house." That answer just wasn't good enough, so I
responded with, "Yeah, but what if I could?" These types of questions
are commonplace for kids, and it's interesting to hear them and see their
short-lived view of the world. It's a mark of growth as we continue to
ask questions throughout our lives, most with what we consider a little
more world-based evidence.

Children filled with imagination lead towards questioning; as you
get older, the questions come not so much from imagination but from
the things you've learned throughout your life. Quick answers and even
nonsensical answers to a child are good enough; there doesn't have to be
much evidence, just something that makes a bit of sense to them. Cows
jumping over the moon are possible in the imagination of a child. Their
original question may have been silly, and a likewise fantastic answer is
usually all that is needed. As we grow older, those types of solutions stop

working. We desire a much more concrete and relevant response to our thought-provoking question, something that can be proven, something factual. It leads us to look for our answers through human thinking. Solutions that may not be readily available, answers that may not have the concrete facts we desire. The critical point where a lot of us give up.

I think everyone at one point or another has reached the ultimate question, which is, "Why does God allow bad things to happen to good people?" We ask this question expecting an answer explainable through our human understanding. We've learned to expect a scientific or factual response. When no solution to this question is immediately available, or the answer to the problem is not what we want to hear, we begin to question our beliefs. Everyone experiences something terrible in their lifetime, or let me correct that, everyone shares what they perceive as something unpleasant. It's easy to point the finger and blame others. It's our human nature to find that scapegoat, that something that caused what we see as something wrong in our lives. Unpleasantness is evident on any given night, on any given news channel. We find it so easy to cast blame that we forget about what it will take to overcome the bad; it's too easy just to give up.

I wrote this book because I faced this question, and I gave up. I turned away from my beliefs and understanding of the existence of God. I spent years wrestling with my faith and understanding of why. In the end, though, I found my answers, and I found them because I finally gave in. I learned I needed God; I knew I needed a relationship with him. I realized that sometimes answers aren't as straightforward as we expect them to be, sometimes it takes time to reveal why. I hope that anyone that reads my story may, in some part, see what faith in God's plan can do for your life and the lives of others. It's not always simple, but it's worth the journey.

CHAPTER 1

AND SO...IT BEGINS!

"Have faith in your journey. Everything
had to happen exactly as it did to get
you where you're going next!"

~ Mandy Hale

It's easy to look back on your life and wish you'd done things a bit differently or dream if only this had happened, then my life would have been so much better. The problem is while we think the "What if's" or "If only" would have made our lives better, we never consider how much that path we took influenced the person and the life we have today. We tend to think that we'd have had a better experience if we'd done things differently. I tend to disagree with this concept. The journey we take each day directly shapes our lives, and even the bad moments are essential as they make us stronger and wiser. It's easy to give up in the face of adversity and take the path of least resistance. The uncomplicated direction may feel right at the time, but it doesn't always fix things. It only masks the problems temporarily. Eventually, you begin to realize the issues are still there, yet you don't know how to deal with them. Many times, this only creates more difficulties, which leads to more conflict, more struggle, more wishing you could go back and do things a bit differently.

Society, over the last fifty years, has taught us to take the path of least resistance. The world that I grew up in trained us to give up.

If you don't like it right now, take an alternate route. If you don't like your marriage, just get a divorce, move on; this will make you a happier person. If you don't want to have a baby right now, just have an abortion; it's your choice; why struggle when you don't have to? If you don't feel like going to church, sleep in, there's nothing wrong with that; it's your life. The list goes on and on. By writing this down, I know that many people will find this offensive because it is their right to do what they want. I don't write these examples to judge; I simply want to show how our society has conditioned us that the easier path is acceptable. When we take the less complicated route, we look at one thing, what's best for us now. We don't consider how the easier decision might affect others or how that decision will affect us down the road. Inattention to these details creates that what-if scenario I mentioned earlier.

I am one of the others that the easier decision of divorce affected. My parents were married very young at the age of nineteen. You see, I was one of those children that were unplanned. I believe my mother became pregnant with me after attending a fraternity toga party while in college with my father. Those were still the days before abortion was legalized in the United States. As a result, my parents decided to get married. My parents were only married for a few short years. I think the struggles of finishing school and their age had a lot to do with their divorce, but that's me thinking now, not as a child. Their easier decision left me with two homes, one of which I only saw infrequently on holidays. Growing up is tough; growing up without both of your parents is extremely difficult. I love both of my parents but resented both for many years. I hated not having my dad around to help me in school, watch me play sports, and offer up fatherly wisdom from time to time. I hated the agony I felt each time I had to board a plane to return home from a visit with my dad. I was a kid; I didn't understand, and I blamed myself.

My parents both remarried a few years after their divorce, which further complicated my feelings. My mother's new marriage only lasted a few years before yet another divorce, and visits to my dad's house felt strange as he and his new wife now had two girls of their own. I felt like I was just a visitor and not part of his family. My mother did her best, but without my father around, I had no real male influences from which to learn. I became very defiant and began getting myself into trouble. I started junior high school with three moves, never staying in any place very long, as my mother was trying to find a new beginning. Each relocation led to more and more confusion, as just as I would get settled with new friends, we would pack up and move again.

I became more and more rebellious as I grew older. My school grades began to drop; Fighting led to several suspensions. I started sneaking around and hanging out with friends that most would consider the wrong crowd. By the time I got to high school, most of my friends were also from single-parent homes. We would get together and spend most of our time experimenting with smoking, alcohol, and drugs. Teenage life became one endless party with no cares in the world. Was it fun? Sure, it was way too much fun! We were a group of boys with a common bond of divorce. We created our path of least resistance as an ongoing party, our escape from the world.

I spent the first three years after high school trying to figure out my path. I didn't want to go to college; in my mind, my time in school was at an end. High school was torture for me, as I just didn't want to be there. My only motivation to go was to see my friends and make plans for the shenanigans that we'd pull after school was over. I spent most of high school with no cares, just existing from day to day. I didn't care about academics, and I didn't apply myself. The only plan I made was a pact with my friends that we'd all enlist in the military. We figured we could get paid to learn a trade, and with the addition of the cool uniforms, we could pick up lots of chicks. No, it wasn't a sound plan, but it was a plan. With that plan in mind, shortly after graduation, I enlisted in the United States Marine Corp. I left a few weeks later for boot camp in sunny San Diego, California.

I was seventeen years old, so I had to convince my mother to sign my enlistment papers. My dad refused as he thought I wasn't thinking things through. He was right. I left for boot camp at the beginning of July 1987. I had never been away from home by myself before but looked forward to this new adventure. Within an hour after landing and being transported to the Marine Corps recruit training depot, my introduction to one of the most chaotic wake-up calls of my life began! It wasn't like the videos we watched at the recruiting station; this was intense, it was real, and it was overwhelming. Looking back now, I still marvel at the creative usage of cussing and mind torture my drill instructors possessed. My journey into the Marines ended in only a few short months. I suffered an injury during training and found myself in Balboa hospital in San Diego, CA. The path I had chosen was not going to work out. A medical separation soon followed my hospital stay, and my plans for a career in the military ended.

I returned home to Tulsa, disappointed and lost. I had no idea what I would do with my life. It didn't take long for me to fall back into the lifestyle I had in high school, living each day just for the party. I took a job in an Italian restaurant, found my friends that were still in town, and jumped right back into all the bad habits I had left behind. My life was going nowhere, my parents wanted me to go to college, but I just didn't want to do anything. I simply existed, got up every day, went to work, then spent the rest of each night drinking to excess, smoking pot, and finding trouble. I completely distanced myself from both my parents and stopped talking to them altogether; I simply had no desire to move forward. I remained in this day to day existence for the next couple of years, slipping into depression and not caring about anything or anyone.

I finally woke up one day and realized my life wasn't going anywhere, and I needed to make a change. I didn't know why this sudden realization happened, but it was so overwhelming I knew I had to find a new path. This change was going to be difficult because the first thing I needed to do was mend a few fences with my parents. Surprisingly they both welcomed me back and expressed that they wanted to help. My father had moved to Louisiana. Since I had never had a chance to live close to him and my two half-sisters, I decided to pack up my belongings and make a move there myself. I felt the only way to move forward was to make something of myself, which would involve going to college. Something I never thought I would do.

It didn't take me long to slip back into the life of the constant party, as I decided soon after entering college to join a fraternity. Now my old life came roaring back but in a much more magnified way. No matter what day it was, no matter what time it was, there was always some kind of party happening at the frat house. I, of course, found myself in the middle of it daily. The fun simply outweighed going to class or studying correctly, so for the first two years in college, I got by. My grades weren't the best, but I passed, and I was okay with that, as long as I could continue with my newfound party ground. This lifestyle continued for a couple of years until I met my future spouse, the new path that I would pursue.

My wife and I met in the spring of 1992, in of all places, a bar. She was straightforward and focused on school but would let her hair down occasionally. She put up with my shenanigans to a point but slowly helped me see that there was more to life than that of the endless party. She was the oldest of five and had a very close relationship with her family. This bond she had with her family was something I had never experienced growing up; it was unusual and hard to understand.

We had only been dating for about a week when she quickly drove down an unfamiliar neighborhood and pulled up to her parent's house. Surprisingly, I sure wasn't expecting to meet her parents yet but followed along as she got out and went up to the door. Her mother opened the door, wearing a bathrobe and curlers in her hair; in one arm, she held a small baby, and right next to her, a vacuum. They handed the baby to me after a brief introduction. Within seconds Donielle and her mother quickly made their way to a back room. I had only held a baby once, and that was on my lap when I was a kid, so I had never honestly held a baby. I stood there for what seemed to be an eternity with my arms outstretched, holding this little smiling baby and silently praying for help. I had no idea what to do. The baby's brown eyes met mine, and I felt a warmth come over me as I'd never felt before, and if I hadn't been so nervous, it might have been consoling.

My wife and her mother came back into the room a few minutes later and burst out laughing at me and the look on my face. It was a look of terror. I handed the baby back to her mom, and eventually calmed down. Looking back on it now, it's funny, but I did not find humor at the moment. Little did I know that would be when I truly fell in love with my wife; she didn't hold anything back from me, not even her baby sister. The awkward moment became my welcome into her family and her life. That moment opened the door to my new path in life, and it was not a path of least resistance.

We continued dating through college and spent a lot of time with her family. My life began to change for the better, but it was a slow process as I didn't want to let go of the crazy lifestyle I had been leading. We had been dating for a little over a year, and all seemed right in the world; unfortunately, though when it looks like nothing can go wrong, it does. We had spent Thanksgiving with her family, and her father just didn't seem himself. He was having problems swallowing his food and didn't eat much. Shortly after Thanksgiving that year, her father went to see a doctor. The news wasn't great; he had cancer of the esophagus. Devastating news for us all, but as all families do in a time of crisis, we banded together. We convinced ourselves that he would beat this thing. During this time, I began to watch the baby during the day to help so that her father could go to his treatments and her mother could continue working. I quickly learned how to take care of a small child; that was the easy part. Watching her dad get worse day after day was a struggle. Observing how each family member dealt with the situation was complicated. Still, the hard part was trying to remain positive for my future wife through all of it.

Sadly, we lost her father a little over a year after his diagnosis. He was only forty-seven years old. It's difficult to put into words how differently death affects a person. My wife bottled her sadness up and became a rock for her family. We both still had a year left in school. Yet, life changed dramatically. We now spent most of our spare time checking in on her mother, babysitting her siblings, primarily the little one, and beginning to plan for our wedding. An extremely stressful time, but we made it. We both graduated a year later. A few months after our graduation, we were married, life seemed to be taking a much more positive turn. We continued to check in on her mother daily and spent more and more time taking care of her youngest sister; this became the norm in our household. What we didn't realize was that normalcy was merely preparation for the future.

We made it through Christmas with her family only to find out a few months later that my wife's mother had now been diagnosed with colon cancer. Unbelievable! It couldn't be happening to us, to this family, again! It took a while for the shock of the news to finally sink in. My wife continued to bottle her feelings, focusing instead on caring for her mother and her siblings. We now spent a considerable amount of time checking on them, running errands for her mother, and taking care of my wife's baby sister Monique. While it was a challenge, it all became second nature to us rather quickly.

Cancer is a mysterious disease that seems to mask the outcome. For several months, my wife's mother appeared to be doing well, and there was hope that she would beat this thing. Unfortunately, hope only lasted a short time. My wife's mother passed away in December of that year at forty-nine; she died only three years after her husband. Our lives changed forever almost instantly. My wife and I took the role of being the head of the family for her brothers and sisters, a challenging task to undertake. My wife's oldest brother lived on his own and took the younger brother to live with him, her middle sister moved in with a family friend, and we took in the baby sister, Monique. Hard to believe we'd only been married about a year and a half and now had a five-year-old, not the traditional way you become a parent. This new path in life that I had chosen had presented me with joy and pain and suffering within just a few years. It would have been easy to give up, go a different direction, but sometimes easy isn't always the best. When you must work harder for what you want, you appreciate it more; sometimes, you just have to give in and realize this is where you belong.

Why is it important to look back? I think it's necessary to look back from time to time to see where we've come from, to look at what we've become. Sure, it's easy to look back and think, if only, or what if, but if things had been different then, I'd be different now. I wouldn't have the family I have today; I wouldn't have the life I have today, I wouldn't be me. Everything that happened during my early years shaped me and taught me. Did I like it at the time? No! Looking back, though, I realize that it had to happen this way to make me who I am. All those choices led me down a path of struggles, but those struggles prepared me for what was to come; facing adversity so young only began laying the groundwork for an exceptional life.

CHAPTER 2

OVERNIGHT DADDY

"For I consider that the sufferings of this
present time are not worthy to be compared
with the glory that is to be revealed to us."

~ Romans 8:18

Who would have thought that just a few years earlier, when I held that little girl in my arms for the first time, that I would now be raising her as my own? Certainly not me! My wife and I had only been married for about a year and a half; we were not even beginning to think about having children. Our plan was something different. The problem is, and this is very hard for most people to understand and accept, our ideas are not always the plan. The plan is what God has laid out for us, the direction he wants us to go in life. Hard to accept because this sometimes interferes with our goals, the route that we want to take. We tend to believe we know what is best. Sometimes we are given gentle nudges towards the path we should take, but occasionally we get a good hard push.

I can not begin to explain the pain of losing a parent, much less both. I watched on the sidelines as this happened to my wife and her siblings. My wife did her best to hide her grief, but she could only hide so much. I had only a short time with both of her parents and grew to love them dearly, and I hurt; I felt lost without them. I just could not fathom what my wife and her brothers and sisters were going through.

Mostly what the baby, Monique, was going through. She was only two when she lost her dad and only five when her mom died. Sadly, I remember a few months after her dad died. We were driving with her near the hospital where he had passed, and she looked up and said in a loud voice, "Daddy's house," as she pointed to the hospital. It broke my heart. All the things we take for granted in this life, especially memories, and this little girl's memory of her dad was his final days in the hospital. How was this fair?

We have all heard the expression, God works in mysterious ways, and he does. We may never truly understand why my wife's parents died so young, but this was part of his plan. Accepting the purpose is something entirely different, and this was the part that was extremely difficult for all of us. I know now, looking back, the grief was hard, but the fear of the unknown was honestly the most troublesome, and I saw that fear in each of her sibling's eyes. My wife and I would have to take charge and become stronger than we knew how because her brothers and sisters needed us to be that strength.

The night after my mother in law's memorial service, my wife and I sat down and talked. It was not a long talk, but it needed to happen. My wife looked at me with tears in her eyes and asked me if I wanted to take Monique and raise her. I was not expecting this question; I had already assumed this is what would happen. I remember answering her right away, yes, I would not have it any other way. Monique had become a significant part of our lives over the past few years, as we had her with us most of the time. From the time her father became sick, we began taking care of her more and more to help, but it became a preparation for this moment. That little girl needed us, she needed a mom and a dad, and we needed her. We will never know why God decided to take my wife's parents at such a young age, we do know that he has a plan, and that plan was for us to raise Monique.

Our lives changed dramatically over the next few weeks as we began to adjust to the situation. We moved Monique into our one-bedroom apartment with us, which became very small overnight. Our couch became a makeshift bed. Our living room transformed into a play area. The overall space became cluttered with toys and boxes of Monique's belongings. Most couples have time to plan for the arrival of their child; our arrival happened overnight. Mixed emotions filled both of us with this new transition. Of course, we were still grieving, but at the same time filled with excitement and questions about the future. How would this work? How would Monique adapt? Would this be too much for her to process?

Surprisingly, small children adapt to situations quickly. Looking back, as much time as we already spent with her, I do not think the living situation was ever an issue for her. She was so young when both her parents died; she did not have time to build many memories. While I have always wished that she had more time to make those memories, in the end, it became a sort of blessing that she did not. Monique did struggle with the situation later, but she seemed to take things in stride as a child. While the new living arrangement felt somewhat natural to us all, it felt awkward when we attempted to explain to other people unfamiliar with what had happened. Explanations brought back memories and grief of losing her parents. Most of the time, compliments and praise would follow the back story of how amazing we were to take her in. We were not amazing; we simply loved her and did what was needed to take care of her. Though not through traditional means, we had become a family.

The first few weeks became a period of adjustment for all of us. New bedtime routines, learning to navigate the maze of toys left around the apartment, and purely getting used to being a family of three and not just the two of us. Life seemed to calm down a bit and a new level of ordinary settled in until I was cooking dinner one night. Monique wandered in, wanting to help, which meant she wanted to play. I continued to cook while taking quick breaks to check on her, play along with her for a few moments, and continuously checking back on the food. Out of the blue, she looked up at me with a big smile on her face and said, "I love you, Daddy." I was stunned and had no idea how to reply, except to say, "I love you, too." To this point, she had always called me Brian and my wife, Donielle. I truly loved her and looked at her as my own, but I never wanted or tried to replace her father.

While her statement melted my heart, it left me with an uneasy feeling. I spoke to my wife later that night and told her the story of what had happened. She told me Monique had done something like that with her the day before, and she had reacted in the same way. We debated how to address this with Monique, but we decided to let it play its course in the end. We felt that the best thing to do was to let her decide what she wanted to call us instead of taking something else away from her. She needed to place ownership of the situation. She needed to be ok with it, and she would have to figure this out independently. We were both ok with whatever she wanted to call us; we had to be for her. Monique attempted to address us as mommy and daddy a few more times over the next few days. Strangely enough, I think she felt awkward and eventually settled back into calling us by our names.

Over the next two years, we slowly began to settle in as a family. Monique started school, which gave her some stability and structure during the week. We made the best of our living arrangements; while it was small for the three of us, it was home. Life came with the typical ups and downs that parents must endure with their children, including sickness. I will never forget the helpless feeling you have as a parent the first time your child becomes ill. There is nothing you can do to make it all better; you try to comfort them, but nothing seems to help, you feel powerless, you feel like you have let them down. What we finally realize once they have recovered is this is a fact of life. You adjust, you endure, you do what you can to make them okay again. I was in sales the first time Monique became ill, and since my job was more flexible than my wife, I stayed home to comfort her. Little did I realize that taking care of a little girl would involve watching endless Barney episodes and reading Cinderella repeatedly. Absolute torture, but I made it. It was after this moment in our short journey together that I felt like a daddy. That was my little girl, and there was nothing that I would not do for her.

After spending several months in the one-bedroom apartment adventure, we finally realized that it was time to upgrade. We needed a house, Monique needed a bedroom, she needed a yard to play in. We decided to begin the process and build a new home. Excitement filled our lives over the next few months as we watched our house form, and finally, the day arrived when we could move in. It felt enormous; it was a castle compared to our small apartment. Our next adventure had come. Our lives began to settle down; we had made it through several difficult moments in just a short period. We were finally a family; we were happy. We can never erase the past; we can only learn from it. Our family had learned plenty over the last five years; we had become more vital. My wife and I had both begun very successful careers; we were now in a new home, Monique was happy. Our family, filled with joy, was now ready to tackle the future. What we did not realize is that our adventure was just beginning.

CHAPTER 3

HEROES

"Without heroes, we are all plain people
and don't know how far we can go."

~ Bernard Malamud

Life seemed to be taking a turn for the better for our family. We were now living in a four-bedroom house with a huge backyard. One massive upgrade from the little one-bedroom apartment in which we had lived. Monique was thriving and active in school and making friends, and she was busy setting up her new room with her toys. Our family life had certainly improved in a few short months. The grief of losing my wife's parents was still present but became more tolerable over time. My wife had become a CPA and had begun her career. I had landed a job in insurance sales; our household income was fantastic. My wife's siblings were becoming adjusted to their new living arrangements and seemed to be doing well. Our future looked bright, and it looked as if the bad times were behind us. We had a positive outlook, dreams, and aspirations of a bright future.

We did the things all young couples do, such as hosting get-togethers at the house, usually a bar-b-que with friends and family. We worked in our off time in the yard to create a beautiful curbside appeal to greet us as we returned from long days at work. We played outside with Monique, as there was room to run and roam in our backyard.

Everything was going the way it was supposed to, and then it got just a little better. We had only been in our home for a few months when my wife presented me with the news that she was pregnant. What an exciting moment, receiving the information that you would soon have an additional member of your family. We were beyond ecstatic and could not wait to tell Monique the news. She would finally be a big sister. Looking back, I think that Monique was more excited than the two of us.

Nothing but pure joy filled our household over the next few months. We all jumped into work on the new baby's room to make it look just right for his or her arrival. My wife and I could not wait to find out the baby's gender and soon received the news; we would be having a baby boy. I was on top of the world! I would have a son; he would be my big football star; I would get to show him how to throw a ball, how to ride a bike, how to fish. I knew I could do all of that with Monique, but there is just something different in the bond of a father and son, something I was genuinely looking forward to having. My wife and I began to talk about favorite names, plans for his arrival, and plans for his future. Our list looked pretty good.

Having our first biological child came with some anxiety. You want nothing more than your child to arrive into the world in good health, with no complications. We both attended each check up on pins and needles, hoping for good news each time, which we received. Our son was growing and preparing to introduce himself to us soon, and we became more and more prepared with each passing day. We finally decided that his name would be Logan; it just clicked with both of us. The name was not biblical; neither of us had any relatives with this name; it had no significance except that we both fell in love with the name the first time we heard it. To us, the name Logan was memorable, a name that you would not forget; it was perfect.

Logan's day finally arrived. I had fallen asleep on our couch in the living room, only to be awoken by my wife in the early hours of the morning, letting me know that her water had broken. We needed to go to the hospital. My adrenaline went into overdrive as I raced around the house to secure overnight bags, Logan's car seat, and Monique. The day was here! I quickly called one of our relatives to meet us to pick up Monique before racing off to the hospital. It is challenging trying to remain calm enough to drive in this excited state. Imagine a small child on sugar overload bouncing off the walls. In my case, it was only about a third of what I was experiencing. Thankfully, the grace of God cleared a path for me and allowed us to arrive safely.

Finally, we entered into our birthing room, nothing special, just space and bed where she would give birth, and we would welcome Logan into the world. A nurse came in to perform a final ultrasound, which showed that Logan would be a big baby, and everything she told us looked good. My wife's contractions began to increase, which became a scary situation for me. Soon to be, fathers must realize that the words that come out of your wife's mouth at that point come from extreme pain; you are not the evil she describes you to be at that moment. The nursing staff finally came in to administer an epidural to relieve some of my wife's pain. I can only describe a woman receiving an epidural like the wolfman's old black and white episodes. The change happens right before your eyes! The relief is almost instant and dramatic, not just for your wife but also for you. I can not begin to understand the pain she was going through. I can only explain the relief I felt as her fingers, which she had dug into my arms, slowly relaxed; it was marvelous.

No one can prepare you for the long labor, the anxiety, the excitement. You feel like a small child waiting for Christmas morning to see the gifts that Santa had delivered. I wanted nothing more than to take the pain away from my wife but could only give her words of comfort as she began to push. Finally, Logan arrived. Experiencing your child's birth is truly unique, but unfortunately, this moment turned into a nightmare within seconds. The doctor pulled Logan out and gently placed him upon my wife's stomach. Logan did not look right; he was grey. I was expecting the doctor to allow me to cut the umbilical cord, but instead, he snipped it quickly. I was expecting the doctor to spank him on the rear, and we would hear him cry out for the first time, but instead, a team of nurses rushed in and took him to a unit across the room.

Time seemed like it stood still. I felt like my heart had stopped; I could not catch my breath. I stood beside my wife motionless, almost paralyzed. I could hear my wife crying and asking me over and over, what's wrong, what's going on, where is our baby? I had no words, only the worst thoughts. Finally, after what seemed an eternity, we were given some relief as we heard Logan cry out for the first time. I knew he was alive; I just didn't know anything else; I had no answers for my wife. Our fears only escalated as the nurses quickly whisked Logan out of the delivery room, to where we had no idea. The doctor calmly finished cleaning my wife up. He looked at both of us and said in a very calm voice, "Don't worry, everything is going to be fine; I'll get some answers for you shortly."

Questions, fear, and concern began to pound in my head. The sound of the world and the realization that time still existed came rushing back into the room. I now began to hear my wife's cries. I felt the panic in her voice, I sensed her fear, but I still had no words. I faced her, tears in my eyes, with an overwhelming feeling of failure, but with nothing to comfort her. I attempted to choke back the tears but to no avail. I grabbed the side of the bed for support as I felt as if I would pass out. I felt helpless; I felt empty. I could not provide any comfort for my wife; I simply couldn't move or breathe.

When I finally regained the ability to move and speak, I began frantically asking questions, but with very few answers. The nurses would only tell me that a doctor would be in shortly. It felt as if my wife and I had become nonexistent, which only added to the fear and frustration. I had nothing to give to comfort my wife. Time went by with no answers, only fueling our worst fears. Was Logan alive? Was he going to be ok? Where did they take him? The moments after childbirth are supposed to be happy and full of joy; these moments for us had transformed into the worst dream imaginable. Finally, a nurse explained that Logan was now in the neonatal intensive care unit. She couldn't explain why but told us that a specialist would come in shortly to provide some answers. Specialist! Neonatal Intensive Care Unit! These were not the words we were hoping to hear. We immediately asked if we could see Logan if we could hold him, but we were only informed no, not at this time; the specialist will explain soon.

The specialist eventually arrived and motioned me over to talk with him. I felt numb as I attempted to walk the short distance. The specialist was of some foreign descent, which made our conversation more difficult. I could barely understand everything he began to tell me, between the words I had never heard before and his accent. All I remember hearing were the words, Spina Bifida, surgery, death, and possibly paralysis in that order; please sign here. I had been given answers but was still very unclear, so I asked for clarification. Logan had been born with a neurological defect called Spina Bifida, and he would require immediate surgery. With any surgery, there is always a chance of death. There was a possibility of paralysis, but to what extent they couldn't tell me. The news was not good, but at least it was news. I walked back over to my wife and relayed the information as best as I could. We both cried; we both felt helpless.

Eventually, my wife and I were taken to a recovery room to wait for the neurosurgeon to arrive to perform Logan's initial surgery. My wife was extremely weak from the birth and the added stress of the situation and desperately needed some time to rest. Unfortunately, there was no way to relax until we knew Logan would be ok. We finally spoke to the neurosurgeon, who explained that an area on Logan's back had never wholly formed, and the surgery would be to close the opening. We still didn't understand the extent of what was happening, but we knew he needed the surgery, so we consented. Nothing seems to move in a hospital very fast; it seems like time goes in slow motion, especially while you're on the outside waiting. The wait for news of successful surgery for Logan was agonizing. We wanted to see and hold our child, we needed to touch our baby, but this couldn't happen. We could only wait, wonder, and hope.

Hours later, we received good news. Logan's surgery had gone well, but with the quick procedure's additional trauma, he would need to stay awhile in the Neonatal Intensive Care Unit. A nurse came in a short while later and informed us that we could see Logan for the first time. Sadly, my wife was still fragile and was finally able to rest with a little help from some medication. She would be unable to go. I went alone to see our son for the first time. I could only stay a few minutes and could not get close enough to touch him; the visit was both comforting and agonizing. Logan was a big baby, and here he lay on his belly in the middle of a dozen premature babies. He looked like a monster. The nurses had already nicknamed him Bubba. There were so many wires and tubes hooked up to various machines connected to his little body. He also had several bandages, I assumed from the surgery, and looked very bruised. During his first twenty-four hours on earth, it looked as if my little fighter had just gone toe to toe for the world's heavyweight championship. It was heartbreaking. It did, however, give me some hope that I could take back to my wife.

The next day my wife and I were both able to visit Logan. A day and a half after his birth, my wife was finally able to see him for the first time. The visit was once again torturous as we gazed at him lying motionless in a little glass cube connected to all those machines. My wife managed a smile for the first time as she glanced at the piece of masking tape where the nurses had written his nickname, Bubba. We still could not touch him or hold him; we could only be there with him for a short time and tell him how much we already loved him. Logan would have to stay in the hospital like this for the next two weeks. We made arrangements for my wife's stay in a room at the hospital for that time while I had to go back to work and explain what was going on to Monique. More hope-filled each day as we watched him improve, and after the first week, we were able to hold him for the first time.

A week later, we finally were able to take Logan home with us, knowing that many struggles still lay ahead. We both had so many concerns, questions, and fears. How were we going to do this? How much more could our family take? All my hopes and dreams for my son were gone! I wanted to fix him, but I couldn't. I wanted this to go away, but it wouldn't. The only thing I knew for sure was that I loved my son. I was in awe of what he had already been through in his short life. He was a fighter! He had already faced challenges in the first two weeks of his life that most of us never have to face, and he cruised through them. He was special. I had no doubt he would make his mark on this world. On May 24th, 1998, I met my son for the first time; little did I realize my hero had also made his introduction.

CHAPTER 4

WHEN A TREE FALLS

"The same boiling water that softens potatoes hardens eggs. It's all about what you're made of, NOT your circumstances."

~ Unknown

I'm a big history buff and love to read stories of old battles. I try to imagine what could have been going through each of the soldier's minds as they marched off to fight with an enemy they did not know and the thought that they may or may not return home. I try to imagine the poor innocent farmers and families that lived around the battle site. The fear that must be racing through their minds as fighting raged across their lands and through their homes. I try to imagine what the children could have been thinking, the sheer terror they felt, as they witnessed the carnage. None of them asked for this, not the soldiers, not the inhabitants of the area. There was nothing that any of them could do but face the battle. Once the fighting had ceased, they now faced the further task of trying to pick up and move on with their lives. Weary, injured soldiers faced the long trek home, knowing they might receive the call again to fight another day, a fight in which they could not object. Families faced rebuilding homes, burying the dead, caring for the wounded, and continuing life knowing at any time the conflict could return, of which they were helpless to prevent. How did they deal with the sadness, the fear, the anger? How did they make sense of it all?

There is an old saying that if a tree falls in the forest and no one is around, does it make a sound? That's what I imagine those soldiers and farmers must have thought following the battles. Does anyone else know what just happened? Do they care? They, of course, witnessed everything up close, but what about the rest of the world? How empty they must have felt knowing that they were the only ones that could truly understand or feel the pain and misery of what had just transpired. For whatever reason, they witnessed the tree fall and heard the sound. No one else felt their pain. No one else understood their fear. No one else could understand their outrage.

Now that we had Logan home, two weeks after his birth, reality began to set in. I now understood and knew what those soldiers and farmers must have felt. I felt like our trees had been falling for several years, but no one was around to listen. I knew my wife had to be going through the same realization, but at this moment, she focused on only Logan. We didn't talk about the situation; we just did. We were the only ones who understood what the other was going through, but we remained silent. In hindsight, it was our way of handling the grief and anger while disguising our true feelings around Monique. While this was difficult enough for the two of us to accept, we couldn't imagine what the reality of this would do to her. We kept our feelings buried and dealt with them in our way as we kept moving forward into the unknown.

Our new ordinary over the next few years involved further surgeries, therapy visits, and countless doctors. It was agonizing to watch your child struggle to do so many things we take for granted. Logan had limited feeling below his waist. Which meant we had to adjust to catheterizing him four times per day to help him empty his bladder along with changing his diapers. Temporary or permanent, they couldn't tell us. As they mature, we see small children accomplish things such as sitting up by themselves or pulling themselves up on all fours. Logan struggled with balance, which meant simple things would not happen for him until much later than a typical child. We knew he had a long road ahead and with each passing day, we felt further prepared to take this journey with him. Our glimmer of hope was Logan's personality; he simply melted your heart immediately. Logan was graced with deep blue eyes and seemed to learn to use them to his advantage almost immediately. He wore a smile from ear to ear like a badge of honor throughout each day. I may sound biased, but he was an adorable baby. Sadly though, people, in general, tend to see our limitations before our gifts.

Our friends and family slowly drifted away as I think the situation completely scared them. I remember confronting my mother about her absence in our lives. She had regularly visited Monique before Logan's birth, but now we hardly saw her. I became angry and asked why? I'll never forget her answer, as she told me she was scared that Logan might die and she wouldn't be able to handle it. What about me, mom? What do you think something like that would do to me? Her statement hurt for a long time, only adding to my outrage. It was never the same between my mom and me after that moment. Many of our friends had children very close in age to Logan, and initially, they would bring them over to visit after we were able to bring him home. As the months went by and their children began talking, crawling, and pulling up into standing positions, Logan still struggled to lift his head by himself. It became very awkward for our friends and us. We wanted to share in their joy of their child's new accomplishments, but we just couldn't. You just don't know what to say when you have never been through an experience like this, you don't know how to act, and I think this is true on both sides. My wife and I understand that distancing themselves from us was their way of handling and coping; everyone has their way of doing that. Unfortunately, we realize that now, years later, when it was happening, though, it only compounded our frustrations as we felt abandoned. Our need for socialization came through work and Monique's sports. These were adults who didn't know us but provided enough adult contact to move forward. We did continue ahead and made the best of the new normal for our family. Still, both of us continued to remain silent about our feelings and dealt with them independently.

Over the next few years, we settled into daily routines and family life. Monique never missed a beat and assumed her role as big sister almost immediately. Logan would make strides, but with each positive, we learned to expect the negative. Acceptance of each new assistive device or further complication for Logan became very hard for me. My wife seemed to take it all in and just move forward. However, I just became angry, refusing to believe that this would be my son's life; I was in denial and was only looking at his limitations. I worked on the road out of town. Much of the information about Logan came to me secondhand as visits to doctors and therapists generally fell on my wife. Secondary information loses its impact. Your questions and concerns are difficult to adequately address as the information is still new to the person delivering the news. You simply must rely on the knowledge handed down and attempt to make sense of it, which only added to my frustration and anger. I couldn't accept the slow pace of Logan's development; I couldn't take the doctors telling us that he would need a wheelchair. I couldn't understand why this had to happen to him.

I entered a very dark place in my life, full of anger at the world, full of anger towards God. I stopped going to mass with my wife; I wanted nothing to do with the church. I couldn't understand how a loving God would allow so much tragedy and grief to happen to one family. If God wanted to punish me, I could completely understand that but not my family and not my son! God saw everything and heard everything, so why couldn't he hear my tree when it fell? If he did hear it, why was he ignoring me? At first, I tried to pray, but I felt so alone, almost as if I were praying into an empty cave. I felt no comfort, I felt no relief, I felt nothing but anger, so I gave up. I walked away from God; I refused to acknowledge his existence anymore. Nothing seemed to matter; I felt numb. I allowed the rage to build until I could do nothing but explode. My outbursts became destructive, breaking and throwing things, anything to release the poison that had built inside me. Blind rage would overtake me; I couldn't focus, I would lose control.

My wife and I fought regularly. I was always irritated over the smallest things. I woke up angry and went to bed in the same state of mind. Our fights became ugly and loud. My breaking point came one afternoon after fighting most of the day with my wife. The argument became so intense, so ugly; she knew she needed to leave with the kids. My rage erupted and resulted in the destruction of our dining room table. When I began to calm down and see what I had done, feel the pain in my hands from scrapes and open wounds, I broke down. I curled up and cried for hours until I finally decided to clean up my mess which was more than the broken table. I need to fix the chaos that became my life, the wreckage I had created through my anger. I decided to sit down with our parish priest and talk. I needed some answers. I needed God.

The priest and I talked for hours about my feelings and my questioning of God. He helped me by asking me a question, "Why do you think God allows good things to happen?" That question caught me entirely off guard. My answer was that if God is all-loving, then why would he allow the unpleasant things? Shouldn't he only let good things happen all the time? The priest followed this question with, "What do you see as bad things?" Well, both of my wife's parents died way too young and left their children with nothing but grief; I think that's kind of harsh. The priest responded, "Do you think it's a bad thing to die and enter into paradise where there nothing but joy?" Well, no, but to die so young and leave those children behind, that's what is painful. The priest explained that what we see as bad things, such as losing a parent, is what we consider bad because of our grief and its impact. But what about Logan? Why would God allow him to suffer? Why would God create him with so many needs, so many struggles facing him? He answered by asking me if I knew what God's plan was for Logan. I could only shake my head and say, "No." We ended our conversation with him, asking me, "Why not embrace what he has in store for Logan, instead of questioning his plan?" I left our meeting, still angry, still confused, but with a door opened. It was time to start again talking to God, I couldn't do this alone, and I'd proven that I needed God's guidance to make this work.

Nothing happened overnight. I won't sit here and proclaim a miracle. What did begin to happen after that meeting was I began to pray, to talk to God. It felt like a one-sided conversation for the longest time until I looked at how I was praying. I was always asking for God to intervene, make things better, and ultimately it was a very selfish prayer.

That's when I began asking God to guide me, just to reveal his plan and give me clarity, to understand and accept things as they were. I also began attending mass regularly with my wife, which I know shocked her. I needed God's presence. Slowly, I started to see things differently. I felt my anger begin to subside. The hot-tempered arguments with my wife began to diminish. My life became much more focused; my purpose became clear. I started to accept things as they were instead of questioning why they had happened.

Roughly a little over a year after my meeting with our priest, our family seemed happy. We had decided to move to a larger home with more room, Monique was doing well and making friends, and Logan had entered school. That's when God decided to give us a new gift, as my wife was now pregnant again. It had been almost seven years since Logan had been born. My wife and I thought our days of having children were over. We felt that God knew we had a lot on our plate, so we had grown content, thinking we would never have another child. That's not what God's plan was, though. We were all over the moon, excited about our new addition to the family.

Logan had a fascination with firefighters around that time and decided we should name the baby Fireman Jacob. He would tell all his friends and anyone who'd listen that he was having a baby brother named Fireman Jacob. Joy filled our home, but that came with a small cost. After having a child born with special needs, my wife and I became very nervous about this pregnancy. I remember my wife breaking down several times with the thoughts of having to go through this again, meaning the struggles we'd been through with Logan. We had the doctors do more tests than usual, paying out of pocket since insurance wouldn't. We wanted to be sure. Thankfully, God gave us another baby boy a few months later; he was completely healthy; we were overjoyed. No, we did not name him Fireman Jacob; we called him Lucas.

CHAPTER 5

WHEN DO I GET TO PLAY?

"Trust in the LORD with all your heart and
do not lean on your own understanding."

~ **Proverbs 3:5**

Logan began school in a special education classroom. He had
orthopedic issues that limited his mobility and forced him to
move around in a small wheelchair. Logan had been in physical therapy
since he was little and could take steps using a walker, but this was
very labored. He was only capable of this for short periods. He still
had limited control of his trunk, which caused balance issues that
further complicated his walking. Logan's growth and development was
anything but typical. He suffered delays with his speech, but through
years of therapy, he was able to communicate. The occupational
therapist worked with us to teach him ways to adapt to his surroundings
and overcome his disability limitations. To further complicate things,
Logan also suffered delays in his cognitive abilities, which hindered
his capacity to understand things at a typical pace. With all these
complications in front of him, we were anxious about how he would do
in school. Would he succeed?

Thankfully, we gained an introduction to the world of special
education. Society conditions us to assume that all children learn in

the same way, typical growth and progress rates. Until you have a child with special needs, you don't realize that regular growth rates are next to impossible. Imagine two children running a race; the first one runs the race with a straight and paved track to the finish line. The second must navigate numerous obstacles uphill on one foot over rocky terrain to get to the end. Which one do you think will finish first? The second child can complete the race, but not at the same pace, not in the same way as the first. There is a plan designed for your child in special education, tailored to their strengths and weaknesses. The plan establishes goals for their learning rate; accommodations and modifications are put in place to help them succeed, the extra help they need. Failure is the last thing you want your child to face, especially after the years of struggle they have already encountered to this point. Logan had to work harder, it would take him longer, but he could succeed in the end.

My wife and I were not only concerned about how Logan would make progress academically, but we also worried about his acceptance by the other children. Logan rarely had play dates since he had so many limitations. Logan couldn't run or climb as the other kids did, so playdates generally resulted in him sitting on the side observing the other children and talking with the adults. He was very social and would speak with anyone who would listen. The problem was that small children wanted to run and play, and Logan couldn't do that. He needed friends, children the same age with whom he could talk to and play. Entering school should help provide that, but it could also expose him to teasing by the other kids. We knew that kids were curious, they haven't developed filters yet, and questions and comments are sometimes rather blunt. Kids will many times go up to someone overweight and say, "You're Fat!" They don't do this because they're mean; they do it because it is an observation. They're kids; they don't have to be politically correct; comments like this just happen. Unfortunately, we knew we couldn't always be at his side, and he would have to learn how to deal with those comments on his own.

Logan quickly assimilated into school. He would come home each day with such excitement, wanting to show us all that he'd been working on that day. Logan made friends, both in his special education classroom and in the regular classroom. He brought home extra papers each day as he enjoyed playing school in the evenings and doing additional work. Our concerns were still that as his progress was slow. We knew his teachers pushed, and Logan would continue to advance, only at a slower pace. He liked being a part of the school; he wanted to do all his friends' things, even riding the bus home in the afternoons. For the first time, we saw that Logan didn't look at himself as disabled. Logan was just like everyone else. He even began to receive invitations to birthday parties from his new friends. However, Logan still spent most of his time on the side as they played games outside, involving climbing, running, and sometimes swimming. Though his difficulties kept him from certain things, he never seemed to be bothered by it, he only wanted to be included, and now he was.

My wife and I spent a great deal of time with Logan, through therapies, doctor's visits, and working with him at home, but we always made time for the other two. One of Logan's favorite things to do was going to his big sister's games, particularly softball. We were never sure what he enjoyed more, watching her play, or visiting with the adults in the stands. He seemed to know everyone at each game, and they all certainly knew him. We would arrive, and he would immediately wheel off in the direction of someone to begin a conversation. His desire to visit others gave us a break to focus on Monique and the baby. We would keep him in our sights out of the corner of our eyes but spent many evenings being able to relax and visit with other adults ourselves.

One night, Logan decided to wheel over next to us in the stands. He was closely watching the game instead of having conversations with the other spectators. I asked him if he was ok, and he smiled and said yes, he was just watching the game. We didn't think much of it at the time. Multiple innings went by, and Logan was still there, watching closely, being very quiet. I again asked if he was ok, but Logan gave me the same response, so I left it alone and continued to watch the game myself.

Monique's game was coming to an end, and Logan had picked up a conversation with a lady sitting in front of us. We were concentrating on the game as it was in the last inning, and we had the go-ahead run on base. The stands were relatively quiet with anticipation as one of our big hitters stepped up to the plate. Suddenly, Logan looked up at me with his big blue eyes and asked me the most challenging question I've ever had to answer. He asked, "Daddy, when do I get to play?"

There was dead silence in the stands; I could feel everyone's eyes on me at that moment; my mouth became dry as I was searching for the words he needed to hear. I think God listened to my tree fall at that moment because there was a swift crack of the bat, and the crowd went wild as the batter had just crushed a home run to win the game. The excitement gave me a few moments to collect my thoughts. I knew I couldn't ignore his question; he wasn't going to give up; he would ask again. Sadly, I had no idea what to say. How could my son ever play baseball? He didn't have the best coordination; he couldn't run; I didn't even know if he could hold a bat. I wasn't about to tell him he couldn't do anything. That wasn't going to happen. I looked down at him and said in a calm voice, "I don't know, but daddy's going to look into it for you."

That bought me some time, but that's all it bought me. Logan wouldn't give up; he would ask again. He needed to play sports. He needed to be part of a team, just like everyone else. Neither my wife nor I had ever considered this. We focused on his development, but we overlooked his desire that most kids have to be part of something. The problem was there was nothing set up to enable kids with limitations to play team sports. The only thing available in our area was Special Olympics for his age, which was only two days out of the year. Later that night, my wife and I began to discuss what we would do, how we would answer him. We knew we had to find something; we had to figure something out. I went to bed that night with a little worry but also a smile on my face. You see, I've always thought that God enjoyed an excellent practical joke here and there. As I lay down in bed, all I could hear in my head that night was a burst of quiet laughter and a faint whisper, "Surprise!"

The next few days were very stressful as my wife and I began to research sports programs that may be available for children with special needs. The internet was still relatively new, and surfing speeds were prolonged, making the task incredibly difficult. There had to be something; we just knew it. We couldn't be the only ones that had ever encountered this with their child. Luckily, God gave us a reprieve as Logan came home from school one day with excitement and handed me a flyer. The flyer was an invitation to attend a scouting night at his school to learn more about becoming a cub scout. "I want to do this!" He told me. I couldn't say no, so I agreed that we'd go check it out and see what it was all about.

I was still worried he wouldn't be able to participate but tried to remain hopeful. We went to the meeting a few nights later and listened as they told us all about scouting, showed off their uniforms, and even showed us a few projects that the pack had done in the past. Logan could barely contain himself as he was certainly ready for this new adventure, but I still had my doubts. I pulled the pack master off to the side after the meeting was over and explained Logan's limitations to him. I asked if he thought Logan would be able to join and become a cub scout. The pack master quickly assured me that the scouts work with all kids, even kids with disabilities, and he had no doubt Logan would be able to do it. That was all I needed to hear and signed Logan up that night; he would be a cub scout; he was going to belong to something.

The next week we purchased his new uniform and book that he needed and prepared for our first den meeting. I had a neighbor sew on his patches, and we were ready to go. The night finally came, and to my surprise, we would be meeting at a house only a few blocks away. We arrived at the place to meet our first obstacle. We looked at the home built on a small hill, the driveway packed with cars forcing us to park in the street. The only way to get Logan to the front door was going up three sets of steps, not the easiest thing to do in a wheelchair. I improvised and decided to carry Logan up the steps first, got him inside the house, then returned to retrieve his wheelchair. We had further difficulties fitting the wheelchair through the front door. Of course, their home interior design set up for typical traffic made navigation around furniture difficult for Logan. We learned an important lesson that night. While the scouts would work with Logan, Den mothers and other leaders did not understand the difficulties we faced, simple things we take for granted. For future meetings, I would need to do some homework to make things go as smoothly as possible for Logan.

Unfortunately, future den meetings continued to present further difficulties. I would call ahead and attempt to suggest rearranging the meeting place so that Logan could quickly get around. We would arrive to see none of the changes done or changes that were not enough. I knew this was causing frustration, not just for me but also for each of the homeowners we visited. The den meetings quickly became very uncomfortable. Pack meetings with all the dens at a neutral site were no better. Our first big pack meeting was at an indoor miniature golf course. I had taken Logan to play miniature golf before, and while he was no pro, he was able to hit the ball and play the game. When we arrived, we found that each of the course holes was bordered by two by four frames, making navigation in a wheelchair impossible. We salvaged the day by sharing a snow cone and convincing ourselves that the next one would be better.

Pack meeting number two arrived at an indoor ice-skating rink. I knew that Logan couldn't skate but felt optimistic that we could at least go on the ice with his chair. I was wrong; this wasn't allowed by the ice rink. We spent the meeting watching the other scouts skate. The announcement of our final pack meeting came through an email, which further disheartened me. The plan for the meeting was to go on a nature hike through wooded terrain. We didn't own off-roading wheels that could be switched out on his chair, so once again, another fail.

I didn't blame the scouts; the leaders didn't understand our situation as they planned their overall pack meetings. They wanted to include us; they just didn't know-how. I knew we couldn't continue with the scouts the way we were; there had to be something else. I wasn't giving up. My son had asked me when he would get to play. I was going to make that happen one way or another. There was no reason he couldn't be a scout. I just had to find the way, which meant scouting with accommodations. Over a few weeks, I began discussing the situation with two other fathers of children with special needs. They both had the same interest in having their sons become scouts. We were familiar with what they needed to succeed. We had a plan. Now we just needed the scouts to understand and accept what we were about to present them.

CHAPTER 6

THE TEDDY BEAR

"Every heart sings a song, incomplete,
until another heart whispers back. Those
who wish to sing always find a song."

~ **Plato**

Logan never had problems with making friends. He always made an impact on everyone that he met. His personality lights up every room and those that are around him. My wife and I had so many concerns once he entered school. Still, over time those initial fears began to subside as we watched his natural charisma emerge. While his struggles through academics remained, he approached each day with positivity and excitement. Early on, we learned that even though God had asked him to live a life with a heavy cross to bear, he had blessed him with an absolute sense of love for life and those around him.

Parents tend to overlook the numerous opportunities available in elementary school to drop in and see their child within their element. Yes, it is time away from work, but you gain simple small glimpses of how your child goes about their day. You get to meet the people they see and interact with regularly. These moments assist in diminishing the anxiety a parent feels with separation from their small child. These opportunities become extremely important for families of children with disabilities. The joy I would experience each time I visited Logan at school would last for weeks. Even though my worry about his future remained, I saw his happiness, which gave me a sense of peace.

Early on, my visits to his school came with a purpose. I wanted to know why his academic progress was behind the typical students and what I could do to help. I had not accepted that Logan's delays might be permanent. In my ignorance, I believed that just by pushing him harder, we could fix things. My focus continued to be on what I considered normal and not on the reality that I witnessed every day. I didn't realize there was nothing to be fixed; Logan was who he was, a perfect image and likeness of God. These visits to Logan's school became God's way of showing me the true blessings he had given to my son.

Logan was in a special education classroom for a big part of his day, surrounded by several other students with various levels and types of disabilities. Each visit to this classroom showed me small glimpses of pure joy and happiness. No matter what each student's disability was or how severe, each of them wore smiles from ear to ear. They loved being with each other, they loved being at school, and it showed. Logan was very attentive to each of them, always working the room and ensuring that he showed attention equally. He had made several friends since he began school, both from this classroom and from the typical classrooms he attended for the remainder of the day. One friendship, though, became very evident to us almost immediately.

Peyton was a young girl in his special education classroom who had down syndrome. She also happened to be non-verbal and had mobility issues, and like Logan, she made her way around through the use of a wheelchair. Her movements were minimal, and most of the time required an aide to get from place to place. They spent a big part of each day together, not only in the classroom but also on their bus ride home. Logan had established a special bond with her over time, even nicknaming her Pae-Pae. It was incredible to see how they would both light up upon seeing and interacting with each other. Every evening Logan would give us full reports of how Pae-Pae was doing. We knew he had a special attachment even before our visits. Honestly, we did not understand how close they had become.

Peyton began to miss a lot of school because of health issues. Logan would keep us updated when Pae-Pae was absent. His demeanor would change each day she missed school. You could tell he was very concerned. One particular day, Logan came home and shared the news that Pae-Pae was in the hospital. He didn't know why; he just knew that she was there and asked if we could see her. We didn't know how to respond. Would her parents be alright with this? How would this affect our son? Eventually, we decided to reach out to Peyton's parents to see if they would consider a visit. My wife spoke to Peyton's father, and both agreed that because of the bond the two kids shared, it would be good for them to see each other. We made plans to see her right after Logan's baseball game that Saturday morning.

Logan's excitement was evident for the remainder of the week. He couldn't wait to see Pae-Pae. We still had our concerns, but we recognized how important this visit was to him. Friday evening came around, and Logan told his mom that he wanted to bring his teddy bear to her. He had made up his mind that it would make her feel better. We tried to convince him otherwise because Logan had received the bear as a Christmas gift. Still, our little guy's determination won us over. We worried that he thought the bear would magically make her well, and selfishly we didn't want him to be disappointed, but we couldn't tell him no.

Usually, Logan was very excited to go to his baseball game, but not this Saturday. His only focus was going to see his friend. You could tell he didn't want to be at the game, but he knew he had to be there and never wanted to let his teammates down. We got through the game, and his eyes lit up with excitement. Finally, we were heading to see Peyton. We arrived at the hospital and made our way to her floor to check in with the nurse. You could see the apprehension in her eyes as we told her who we were there to visit. Peyton had been extremely sick, and only recently, the nurses had taken her off a ventilator. She was beginning to recover but had a long way to go. After checking with her parents, the nurse agreed to allow us in. Logan would finally get to see Pae-Pae.

We went back to her room and found her sitting on her grandmother's lap. Only her father and grandmother were in the room, and Peyton looked so weak. Logan entered with his teddy bear in hand, full of energy and a big smile calling out her name. To everyone's surprise, she instantly perked up a little and began to smile. He gave her his gift, and she hugged it hard. The change in that little girl's face said everything; her joy beamed. The two of them just sat and visited for a while; of course, Logan did all the talking. Peyton's dad looked entirely astonished by what was happening. He told us she hadn't had that much energy in days; he couldn't believe it.

A nurse came in after a while for Peyton's periodic monitor check. Amazingly, her oxygen levels had increased to one hundred percent, something that hadn't happened the entire time Peyton was in the hospital. Logan and Pae-Pae just continued to bask in the presence of each other. Before we knew it, three nurses had entered Peyton's room, marveling at how much energy she now had. Peyton had been in the hospital now for over a week, showing minimal signs of improvement. We could visibly see the initial stress on her dad's face relax with signs of relief. For just a brief moment, we experienced complete joy within Peyton's room.

We left from our visit with Peyton that day with smiles all around. Her dad and grandmother thanked us repeatedly, while each nurse asked Logan to come back soon. I remember getting back to our vehicle for the ride home and marveling over what I had just witnessed. In 1 John 4:12, John writes, "No man has ever seen God; if we love one another, God abides in us and his love is perfected in us." Logan had demonstrated pure love in a way I could not imagine. The simple contribution of a teddy bear seemed so trivial to us at the time. Still, in the end, it became one of the most precious gifts imaginable. The present was only a token; the real gift was Logan's love for his friend.

God demonstrated to me that day why he had created Logan the way that he did. Logan was made different and made for a unique purpose. I had focused on all of Logan's problems and how they had taken away our normal. I wasn't able to see past that until this moment. I began to change after that; I began to look at the world in a completely different way. Logan's wheelchair wasn't the problem; my focus was. Up to that point, all the obstacles blinded me as to what we would face as a family; I couldn't see the true blessing God had given us.

Peyton recovered from her hospital stay and returned to school a short time after that visit. Logan continued to share his special bond with her for years, staying in touch even after they went their separate ways into middle school. Peyton continued with several health issues and unfortunately passed away a few years ago. Logan was heartbroken but insisted on attending her funeral. He had another mission. While he needed to say goodbye to his friend, he also felt he had to be there for her dad. They have remained close to this day. Through a simple act, I've learned never to underestimate the power of love. Just a few precious moments can change lives.

CHAPTER 7

MAKE IT SO

"When everything seems to be going against you, remember that the airplane takes off against the wind, not with it."

~ Henry Ford

Our research into sports programs continued at a slow pace. My wife and I had found a few leads, but to this point, that's all they were. We had some ideas, but we felt we needed some guidance from someone who had experience with these programs since this was new to us. Finding information was extremely difficult. Contact numbers and email addresses were non-existent or canceled. The programs we saw had only lasted a limited time. We went directly to Logan's special education teachers hoping they would have some answers or clues, but they were at a loss. We contacted local disability resources in our local area. Still, all answers revolved around one-day programs through various organizations. We were looking to build something with a season of six to eight weeks. While this was discouraging, we were determined to find something and continued our search in our limited spare time. Something would turn up; we knew it was out there; we just had to look in the right place. Thankfully, Logan and I were making the best of the cub scouts, but if I couldn't make some changes, this wouldn't last long.

One of the side benefits of therapy is that you're not the only family coming each week. Since treatment occurs with the therapist and your child, you have a lot of time spent in the waiting room with other parents and caregivers. Over time you begin to develop relationships with these people and gain a new understanding of their struggles as not all disabilities are the same. I had built two of these relationships over the years with two fathers of children with cerebral palsy. Cerebral Palsy is a neurological disorder caused by brain damage affecting the child in numerous ways, most commonly through muscle weakness and inhibiting motor and movement development. Disheartened by the continued difficulties Logan and I faced while trying to participate in the cub scouts, I began telling them both about the experiences. I had never been in the scouts as a child, but both men had; one of them had attained the rank of eagle scout. We discussed how our children could participate, along with the right accommodations in place. One of the dads suggested that we set up a meeting with the Boy Scouts of America's local office. The gathering would first explain what I had experienced and our desire to see our boys participate in scouting. Mabey they could give us suggestions that we hadn't thought of to this point.

We set up a meeting with the District Director of our local scouting office a few days later. I recounted Logan's experiences and my discouragement with continuing with the scouts. We discussed the various needs that each of our children faced. All parents become familiar with their child's individual needs. We learn how to work with them. We felt that leaders who had never worked with children with special needs had difficulties preparing for meetings that offered full inclusion. All our children were bound to wheelchairs and had similar needs. Still, many other disabilities presented other struggles that would need consideration. We asked for suggestions as to how our children and others with disabilities could participate in the scouts. The District director listened and wrote down careful notes throughout the meeting and mentioned that he had heard of a few packs around the country developed because of similar situations. He would have to contact his main office to get further information but was sure we could figure something out.

A few days later, we received a call from the district director. He gave us the news of approval to form our pack devoted to children with special needs. The information gave us hope and a sense of excitement. We quickly decided that one of the dads would become our pack leader since he had previous experience with the scouts. I would become his assistant. Our next step was to set up an informational night and sign up to begin our adventure. In November of 2006, the Boy Scouts of America officially commissioned Pack 296, to start with six scouts. We partnered with Goodwill of Acadiana, who would supply space for our meetings and help in other areas. We agreed to meet as a pack twice per month, instead of the traditional weekly den meetings, since our group was so small, and we would plan for two to three hours of activities.

We soon began meetings and activities with our pack. The kids were so excited to wear their uniforms and to be a part of something. Our leadership handled accommodations with ease as each of the parents could discuss their child's needs before meetings. The scouts worked on assignments from their scout books and began working towards badges. We developed activities that included camping, fishing, and even a little archery. You could see the pride grow, not just from our scouts, but the parents as well. Unfortunately, our time with our original pack master ended after just a few short months, with his transfer out of state. I took over as pack leader. Our pack began to grow. In only a few months, we had eighteen scouts with various disabilities, including Autism, Downs Syndrome, and some with multiple disorders. I had even inherited two young men, one with Downs Syndrome and the other with Asperger's who had reached the eagle scout rank, who became my assistants. They fully embraced teaching the skills they had learned growing up to our kids.

I would spend hours preparing for each meeting to ensure that we accounted for each scout's needs, which made our time together run a smoothly as possible. The joy and happiness were visible each time we met. One of our newer scouts had multiple disabilities and would always arrive with his parents. He could not walk, had a feeding tube, and spent his day in a large stroller type apparatus. He slept most of the day; I had never seen him open his eyes in the several months that I knew him. I would always ask if there was anything I could do to make his time more enjoyable. I worried that the activities I presented in each meeting were not stimulating enough. His parents always reassured me that everything was fine, and they were thankful that there was something for him to do. During one of our meetings, I happened to look over at this child, and for the first time, his eyes were wide open, he had lifted his head, and he was smiling. I almost did a backflip with my excitement! I thought I was witnessing a miracle at that moment. His parents would explain to me later that it was a special moment as he only opened his eyes three to four times per day. God has such a unique way of sending signs to show you what you're doing is an essential part of his plan. Proof like this one was one moment that will live with me for the rest of my life.

My wife and I were thrilled with how well the establishment of pack 296 was going, but we never gave up on finding other programs. We were determined to bring some kind of sports program to our area where kids with special needs could become part of a team. We seemed to be hitting one wall after another. Finding information on established and tested programs proved very difficult. Sometimes, what you seek is right in front of you the entire time. Monique wanted to play soccer, and my wife noticed when signing her up that there was a listing for TOP soccer. She decided to call and get a little more information on the program. God brings the right people together at the correct times, sort of like finding that one piece of the puzzle that creates an image and makes the picture come alive.

TOP soccer happened to be an adapted soccer program. The program had been developed by a man who just happened to be a soccer buff, always involved in our community soccer leagues. He never had children with special needs, but for some reason, he felt compelled to develop a plan that would allow children with disabilities the opportunity to play the game. He had run it a few seasons in the past, though he only had a few kids that would come and participate.

My wife and I were elated with this news, and my wife made plans to contact him immediately. A few days later, my wife spoke with him about his program and explained our interest. He was thrilled to have additional help. We began working with him immediately on the next season and just a few months later introduced over thirty children with special needs to the game of soccer. The Lafayette Youth Soccer Association allowed us space to play behind their offices, which included a large cemented area ideal for our players in wheelchairs or walkers. They also offered us space to store our equipment throughout the season. My wife's college sorority began sending volunteers out to help, which they did every weekend for the six-week-long program.

That first season was a complete success. Each player was issued a jersey and worked on drills involving dribbling through cones, shooting, and passing for the first half. During the second half, they played a structured game with two sides and our volunteers' help. Our players in wheelchairs were able to use over-sized balls, giving them greater flexibility with kicking. We knew Logan wanted to play, but as we had learned while working with our scouting program for just a short time, we knew that other kids with disabilities would like to play as well. Everyone wants to be a part of something. Through the TOP soccer program, we watched as they all formed friendships, experienced joy, and beamed with pride. Parents had the chance to see their child do something they never thought possible. Our sorority volunteers requested to continue working with us in the future, as so many young women had been changed by simply lending a helping hand to our kids.

The TOP soccer program founder moved to Houston, TX, later for work but agreed to continue his program. He intended to establish his program in the Houston area and planned to stay in contact. We can never thank him enough for introducing our kids to the world of adapted soccer. My wife and I began planning for next season but continued our research into other sports programs. We knew our child well, and we knew he would want to do more. The scouting program was established and running; it had provided us somewhere to start. The TOP soccer program had gotten the ball rolling by giving a team sport in our area for children with special needs. These programs became the beginning of something good for us, we just didn't know what that was, but we felt compelled to continue to look to find the next big thing for these kids. One night our online research finally gave us a glimpse of what was next. I had found something special; what I'd seen was nothing short of a miracle.

CHAPTER 8

DREAM IT. BELIEVE IT. ACHIEVE IT.

"You don't build it for yourself. You know what
the people want, and you build it for them."

~ Walt Disney

We had experienced some success by forming the cub scout pack and working hard to ensure its growth and then finding the TOP soccer program. My wife and I were excited about the new opportunities now available for Logan and many other children with limitations like him. We had continued our research, looking for other programs that would allow additional options, but the process had been slow. One night shortly after TOP soccer had completed its season, I stumbled upon something big, something we had to bring to our community. It was called the Miracle League, which was a baseball program designed for children with special needs. Their motto was what we believed in and precisely what we were looking for, "Every child deserves a chance to play baseball." I felt tears stream down my cheeks as I read about their journey and what they had accomplished. It felt so much like our story, what we wanted to do in our community for our child; he deserved the chance to play. The only question was, how could we make this possible?

The organization operated just outside Atlanta, GA, one of the top ten metropolitan areas in the United States. They documented over 75,000 children with special needs living in this area that could participate in this program. They had the backing of several large organizations that supplied funding to build a field to meet all participants' needs. They had done their homework. They had a place to play, and they had financial backing, they had support. We were still very new to this and only wanted to improve our community for our child and other children with unique needs like him. The thoughts of how we could make this a reality were overwhelming, but I knew we had to get it done.

I shared the information with my wife. We began discussing how we could make something like this happen in our community. The Lafayette, LA area did not have any vast sports complexes at the time. We were limited to baseball diamonds managed by the local parks and recreation department and our local little league fields. We didn't have relationships with organizations that would be willing to provide funding. All we had was desire. The next day my wife arrived home from work very excited. She had continued researching and had found that Little league baseball had an existing program called Challenger baseball. She had already reached the league office requesting the possibility of beginning a Challenger program here in our area. I think we both jumped for joy that night at the thought of this happening sooner than later.

A few days later, we received a call asking to meet with the Lafayette little league board to discuss opening a Challenger division. The board had only one concern: could we find enough kids to play if they set up a Challenger division? Their concern was making sure there was a need in our area for something like this program. My wife reassured them that finding enough kids to play would not be a problem. The board agreed to begin a Challenger division at the beginning of the next season, which was only a few months away. God again was at work. We were going to tell our son he would play baseball just like his big sister. He would be on a team; he would have a uniform; he would finally play. We spent the next few months spreading the word through our community and preparing for opening day.

A few weeks after the Challenger league's approval, I had a minor sinus procedure done with a specialist outside of town. My wife had taken me, and on the return home, we began to talk about the programs that were now available in our area. One of the things we both agreed upon is that there needed to be more. Individuals with disabilities deserved to have the same opportunities for socialization and fun that everyone else did. These opportunities should be available year-round with various options from which to pick and choose. Every individual is unique; they have differences in what they like to do and what they prefer not to do. We knew that we needed financial backing, volunteers, and space to provide future programs. My wife proposed that we create a non-profit organization that would help us in this process. I loved the idea, and we agreed this was the route we would take to further our plans, but we needed a name. We decided to give this some thought; my wife's only request is the word dream had to be part of the identity.

We started brainstorming possible names, but we could not agree on any of the suggestions until I proposed that we just call it the Dreams Foundation of Acadiana. The word itself would be an acronym that stood for Disability Resources Education and Activity Management Services. That was it. That's what we would call our non-profit. The foundation would be a one-stop-shop for information regarding disabilities in our area. We would create, run, or promote sports and activities. We would also help spread the word for what other organizations working with disabilities were doing. We would look for ways to help educate our community. It is a nightmare as a parent to receive a diagnosis that your child has a disability, and finding the right resources and places to help is extremely difficult. There are so many steps that happen as your child grows, so many new obstacles thrown your direction. You need to know where to find the people or resources that can help your situation. We knew this from first-hand experience, and we wanted to help others through those struggles as much as we could.

We filed paperwork to become a non-profit with the state immediately, knowing this might be a lengthy process. The excitement we felt with what we had already accomplished and our new foundation's formation was unbelievable. We began collecting information immediately from various organizations around town. We started setting up a website to help promote the things we were doing. Social media was in its early stages, but we decided to give Facebook a try to create a presence for the foundation. Facebook became an invaluable tool for sharing and connecting with large numbers of individuals within our area affected by some form of disability within their families. Getting information about events, activities, or sharing links to other organizations' sites was efficient and straightforward, which was nothing short of a blessing for us. While we still waited on official approval, our non-profit had begun, we had no idea the impact it would make.

Opening day finally arrived, along with almost thirty players ready to begin the inaugural season. We arrived early to dispense player jerseys and hats. The kid's eyes lit up when they received their very own jersey, and none of them could wait to put them on. It was a beautiful cool spring morning, the smell of freshly cut grass in the air. Our two Challenger teams paraded out on the field for the first time participating in the opening ceremonies with all the other clubs. They and their parents beamed with pride as each team was announced and introduced to the crowd.

The ceremonies closed, and the two Challenger teams made their way to the field to open the season. Each team took their respective dugouts and awaited the umpire's shout of, "Play Ball!" You could feel the electricity of excitement in the players, coaches, and the large crowd of spectators that had come to watch. Some of the players approached the plate as if they were competing in the World Series, going through series after series of gyrations getting ready for their big at-bat. One player walked out, rubbed dirt in his hands, got in position to bat, and took a step back, looking squarely at the coach who was pitching. He held up his arm and pointed up in the air towards left field, reminiscent of Babe Ruth. These kids were having the time of their lives.

Logan's turn to bat finally arrived, but he asked us to bring his walker as he approached the plate. He wanted to bat standing, which meant one arm on the walker for support, the other swinging the bat. I can not express the nervous feeling I had in the pit of my stomach. He steadied himself, lurched at the first pitch and missed, but remained standing. The second pitch traveled over the plate, and he swung, this time hitting a little dribbler down the third baseline. He dropped the bat and took off in his walker for first base. The crowd went nuts, cheering him on as he shuffled forward. His moment had arrived; this was what he had wanted; he was playing baseball. Usually, unless it's a big hit, a player can only take one base, but this wasn't one of those ordinary moments. Logan rounded first base and kept going to everyone's astonishment. He was struggling to put one foot in front of the other, but he wasn't giving up. Tears welled up in my eyes as I watched my son make his way around all the bases and head towards home. There's an old song by the Foo Fighters that reminds me of this moment every time I hear it. "There goes my hero, watch him as he goes. There goes my hero; he's ordinary." Although I always change the last word to extraordinary. Logan made it to home plate for his big home run. He truly amazed me that day with his sheer determination. During this first game, the excitement felt is why we needed programs like this in our community; this is what it was all about.

The fans in the stands certainly got a show that day. They had come in support but received a precious gift. You just couldn't script a better beginning. Parents, players, and coaches were all delighted at the end, all longing to do it again. Several of the board members were also there; the looks on their faces said it all; this was the start of something good. We made the right call. To this day, my wife and I can not thank the Lafayette Little League board enough for agreeing to begin Challenger baseball. That first game was a defining moment in our community. Baseball is just one of those games everyone seems to enjoy and want to play. Most of our kids had spent years watching older brothers or sisters play the game while they sat on the sidelines wishing to do the same thing. Opening day had done two things for us; first, it gave us our answer to Logan's question, and second, it clearly showed us the need for more programs like this in our community.

God smiled down upon that opening season. Every game seemed to be better than the last. We were given beautiful weather each day except for one, which turned into an impromptu snow cone party under tents. The kids didn't seem to mind. The season ended with every player being named an All-Star and given trophies to sport on their shelves. The next season's plans had already begun with talk of traveling to Houston to play in a Challenger jamboree against other Challenger teams. We were heading into the summer months, which becomes incredibly hot and humid in south Louisiana. My wife and I knew we needed to keep the ball rolling; these kids needed something to do during the summer. The question was, what?

We decided to create a bowling league after calling one of our local bowling alleys. They were receptive to the idea and agreed. They allowed us a morning slot every Saturday for our kids to come and bowl and use their bowling ramps for our bowlers in wheelchairs. We wouldn't have to worry about the weather or the heat. All we needed to do was find the kids that wanted to bowl. We sent out news to our growing contact list for registration and watched as we totaled twenty-five bowlers in just a few weeks. Bowling began at the beginning of June that year with seven teams, each with catchy names like the strikers and the gutter rats. We thought bowling would be a completely relaxed environment for our kids. We quickly ran into a few problems, which taught us a considerable amount of patience while finding the solutions. When you begin to work with multiple disabilities, you quickly uncover struggles you are not familiar with and must immediately educate yourself. That first summer of bowling was a little stressful for us. Still, the participants enjoyed themselves in the end, and that's what it was all about for us, their enjoyment. Smiles were our reward.

Approval for our non-profit status came that summer. We could now move forward as an organization. While it was only a start, we had found a way for multiple programs to offer throughout the year for individuals with disabilities. They not only had the opportunities available, but they had choices. We had no idea what the future had in store for the Dreams Foundation; all we knew is we were heading in the right direction. What had started with my son asking when he would get to play, that question had become something much larger. We had quickly fallen in love with each of the kids that had come to participate. We could see that Logan wasn't the only one asking that question. It still amazes me how these programs quickly opened in our community. All we had to do was dream of the possibilities, and we believed in those dreams. The rest was easy; we just simply needed to ask. God had given us another nudge down the path he had laid out for us. We didn't fight it, and we didn't complain, we didn't question it, we only traveled the direction he wanted us to go and look at what happened.

CHAPTER 9

A NEW DIRECTION

"Choose a job you love, and you will
never have to work a day in your life."

~ Confucius

When I was in college, I had my heart set on moving to a big city and landing a job in advertising after graduating. I felt that's where the opportunities were; I thought this was the route I would take. How your life changes in just a few short years. I could not have predicted meeting my wife. When we first began talking about where to live after college, my wife seemed open to the idea of maybe Houston or Dallas. Somewhere close enough where we could still visit her family regularly. That was before her parents died, that was before we had Monique. The series of events that happened over three years quickly changed those plans. How could I take my wife away from her brothers and sister when they needed her most? How could I uproot Monique from taking her away from family after losing her parents at such a young age? I couldn't do that; we needed to be here. Unfortunately, Lafayette wasn't a mecca for the advertising industry. The few jobs in this industry I found just didn't have the potential I was looking for, no real hope of advancement or the future. I still needed to support my family, so I began exploring other options. I finally settled on taking a job in insurance sales; it wasn't glamorous. Still, it would pay the bills right away until I found something else.

The problem I faced very soon after beginning my sales career was that I was good at it. Good money became great money very fast. There are numerous perks in sales and a good paycheck; top salespeople frequently were awarded free trips at the companies' expense. Some of these trips were close, within driving distance. Still, the hotel and food costs were taking care of along with per diem checks to cover any additional spending you might have over your stay. Then there were the big trips; these came with the same extras but were to places like Maui, Scottsdale, AZ, and Quebec, to name a few. I grew very accustomed to these trips over my sales career. You also received bonus money and other surprises the company decided to reward you with for your performance. Recognition is fantastic; awards are lovely, and believe me, the money was incredible. All of this comes with a price, though, that price is time.

You must devote a considerable amount of time on the road seeing clients and potential clients to be exceptional in sales. While this time is convenient for your clients, it may not be favorable for you, which means spending many evenings on the road until very late at night. I also spent many weekends, either on the long trips, making phone calls to set up appointments, or completing paperwork. The price I paid to be a top salesman; was the time I could spend with my family. My wife was growing her business as a self-employed CPA, which meant she had a considerable workload on her plate.

The combination of our two careers began to take a toll on our marriage. We fought constantly. I had no choice about the times I had to be out there; I had to go when other people were home from work. The problem was that my wife now had to face taking care of the children by herself on most evenings and wait from my return to finish work she would bring home. My time on the road also put a toll on my time with my kids. I'd feel sick when I couldn't attend one of Monique's basketball or softball games. Logan and Lucas were usually asleep by the time I'd get back late at night. I spent fourteen years of my life in sales. While the income was fantastic and the benefits tremendous, I physically hated my job because of the hefty price I paid each time I left the house.

That price I paid became larger once we began working with our programs. I was in charge of the cub scout pack, so I had to spend a great deal of time preparing before each meeting. Most of our meetings or games with the sports programs would occur on the weekends, which meant I had to choose where I would spend my time. I felt guilty for either choice I made for multiple reasons. I wanted nothing more than to be with my family. I wanted to be at every game in support of Monique. I desired to be at everything we did through our foundation, but spending more time with the foundation, meant a drop in my income and more pressure to reach quotas. I was miserable.

The two places I felt the most joy was with my family and spending time with the kids participating in our activities through Dreams. I fell in love with those kids almost instantly. What I didn't realize was that other people saw my happiness too. One morning after a thrilling Challenger baseball game, a parent came up to tell me just what she saw. She said she was amazed at how well I worked with each child and made sure to spend time with each of them at each game. Her next question, though caught me completely off-guard, she asked me, "Where do you teach?" She had decided that I must be a teacher based on my interactions with the kids. I remember laughing and answering her, saying, "I can't afford to teach, I make real money, I'm in sales." We both laughed, and she explained that she just assumed I was a special education teacher by the way I worked with the kids. I left the game that day feeling as if her words had complimented me, but also with a nagging feeling that I was missing something.

I put that conversation out of my head and went back to my typical days of being on the road. The difference was I couldn't get that lady's question out of my mind. What did she see in me? What did I do that made her think I was a special education teacher? I was just being me, showing those kids my love, helping them where they were struggling, and just talking to them. I'd try to think of other things to get my mind off it. Still, when you spend a lot of your evenings with windshield time, it became more challenging to think of something else as my mind would always drift back to that question. I didn't talk to my wife about it; I don't know why. I guess I felt a little foolish as much as it bothered me. I began praying about it, asking God to please tell me what it meant; why were those words continuously coming into my thoughts? I received no clear answers.

After months, I finally realized one morning that this was God's way of telling me that's what I was supposed to do, that was part of his plan. I was supposed to become a special education teacher. I remember dismissing the thought; this couldn't be right. I make way too much money to change careers now. I couldn't ask my wife to take a hit like that to our family income. Becoming a special education teacher would mean I would need to return to school, which would be an added expense, and when was I supposed to do that? So, I did what most of us would do; I fought it. There was no way I was going to consider this anymore; this was crazy! I fought with God over this for weeks, guess who won.

I remember going to bed one night and praying, waiting on sleep to arrive, but what came was another question. Where are you most happy? That's when I realized that this wasn't such a crazy thought. I was most happy when I was with the kids in our programs. I was cheerful while I was working with them. My place was with those kids; that's why I was so happy when they were around. God knew this would be a difficult decision for me to make. That's why he had me wrestle with the thought for so long. He had to show me the path he wanted me to take and why I needed to take it. It was clear now; yes, it still sounded crazy, but it was clear what I had to do. Now came the hard part. I had to sit down and discuss this with my wife. I figured she'd probably ask for a divorce, thinking I'd lost my mind. I was petrified to talk to her about it. A change like this would make a dramatic impact on our income, and I didn't know if she'd be on board.

It took me two weeks to build up the courage to talk to her, but it finally happened. I explained everything from the beginning. I explained how much I'd fought with it but that I realized this is what God wanted me to do. My wife laughed at first, not because she found this amusing, I think because it came as a bit of a surprise to her. We had been miserable. Our careers always seemed to get in the way of each other, and we fought regularly. Surprisingly, she took what I had to say relatively well, but the disbelief was still evident. I had never talked about teaching with her before, so it was understandable that she was a little baffled by what I had just laid on her.

We spoke for a long time about it, as my wife had some concerns. Her biggest worry was that I didn't seem to have any patience around the house, especially with our kids. I agreed but pointed out there was something different when I worked with the kids in our programs. When I work with them, I know they learn differently, accept it, and frequently remind myself of it. For whatever reason, I remain calm and empathetic. My wife acknowledged my answer; she knew I was unhappy and had seen how I worked with the kids in our programs. I don't believe she was sold on the idea but knew we needed a change. Mabey becoming a special education teacher was the answer. Even though it sounded crazy, we both decided this was my new path; now, we just needed to figure out how we could make this happen.

I began investigating what it would take to get my teaching certification. There was only one way, and that was returning to college for a while. I would need to complete thirty hours of classes. Returning to school worried me for two reasons. I had never been a great student when I first went to college. I was now forty with three children, not to mention the immediate hit to our income. We had some savings built up, but that would only go so far. I was going to need help. I decided that I would have a conversation with my dad before exploring the route of student loans. My dad was recently retired, and over the years, we had built up a pretty good relationship. I figured that he might lend me the money I would need and allow a long payback time. I was right; after hearing what I had to say and what I wanted to do, he agreed to help. I figured it would take about a year, so we sat down and worked out a plan along with my savings to make this a possibility. The new path was going to become a reality.

I began classes in the fall semester of that year. I was right; going back to school at the age of forty was rough! It took me a while to get into the swing of things but soon found my groove. I had to get used to being that older man in the class, you know there's always one, and I was him. My grades were fantastic as I dove into the material; I wanted to learn everything I could about special education. If I were going to be a special education teacher, I would be a good one. What I thought was going to create additional stress in my household made it calmer. I had more time to spend with my family, and I had more time to spend with our foundation. My wife and I began reversing roles as she now had more time to spend with new clients and build her business. God knows what you can handle and when to introduce new hurdles in your life. My classes went by quickly, and I completed my coursework in just over a year. I had attained my teaching certification, and I was ready for a classroom. A requirement was to spend a semester student teaching, but that lasted only two-weeks. I was immediately offered a job in a non-verbal autism classroom at a local middle school. My time had arrived; I entered this next adventure, knowing that this was God's plan all along. I was now a special education teacher.

CHAPTER 10

SETBACKS

"All the world is full of suffering;
It is also full of overcoming."

~ **Helen Keller**

R aising a child with a disability presents numerous complications and setbacks that most parents of typical children never face. All disabilities are not the same; they each come with unique sets of problems and obstacles that add to the situation's overall stress. Disability, in general, requires time and attention, much more than is needed to raise a typical child. That additional time takes away from time spent with other children and time spent between a husband and wife, all of which can certainly take its toll on the family. Logan had his share of setbacks along the way, and with any setback, you can do one of two things, you can give up, or you can rise up and overcome. We chose to rise up.

Logan was born with Spina Bifida, an abnormality in which the spinal column didn't form properly. He was born with a portion of his spinal cord and nerves exposed. He required immediate surgery to close the area on his back to protect him from further complications. The initial procedure was why he was required to stay several days in the neonatal intensive care unit, as surgery immediately after birth is very traumatic. Logan's first surgery led to his second a few weeks later, as he was diagnosed with having Hydrocephalus. The problem meant that he was building up excessive fluid around his brain. The second surgery required inserting a shunt or tubing into his brain, passing through the skin, helping drain the excess fluid to his abdomen. The shunt design allowed for his growth, but there can be further complications with clogging or infection, which would require changing the shunt at later dates in life. Simple right? Two surgeries in his first months of life.

Children with Spina Bifida may experience incontinence problems as they may not have the ability to control when they go to the bathroom because of the spinal cord exposure. As we quickly found out, a further complication for Logan was that we would need to catheterize him four times per day to empty his bladder. Personally, learning to catheterize my son was one of the most horrific things I've ever had to do in my life. Was I possibly hurting him? That question would race through my head each time I did it. The bladder is not the only issue here; bowel movements are random in occurrence and amount. It seems like you always have a surprise waiting on you throughout the day. I must laugh when I hear new dads explain how they have to get used to changing diapers, especially their reactions to cleaning up after a number two. Guys, you have no idea how easy you have it. Diaper changes with typical children generally last only a couple of years; with Logan, this would be over his lifetime. Accidents happen with every child, but they often occur much more with a child with limited feeling and control. It's hard to understand your frustration as a parent when this happens, especially when your child is older. That feeling is especially true when it occurs in a public place with limited means of cleaning him up. People that haven't experienced this or understand the situation cannot fathom what you're feeling at that moment. Over time, you begin to accept it as a fact of your child's life and can handle it with ease, but it is an embarrassing nightmare in the beginning.

Urinary tract infections became commonplace. Anytime you introduce something foreign to the body, such as a catheter, you risk infection. UTI's at first was scary but easily handled through the administration of antibiotics at home. Like any other sickness, Logan visibly felt terrible and would run a very high fever for several days.

Once the antibiotics ran its course, he would soon recover and be back to his usual self. The problem with the UTI's was the frequency they would occur. It seemed like he would have a UTI at least three times per year, even as careful as we were in our attempts to provide a sterile environment for his catheterization. Prescribed antibiotics are fantastic and will usually fight off the infection. Your child will be great in a few days unless you begin to have multiple contaminations. Multiple uses of the same medicine over time begin to show ineffective results. You must now use more potent medication to fight off the infection, which must be administered through an IV and monitored by medical staff.

My wife and I had one of our first experiences with an extended hospitalization for a UTI infection while traveling to Mexico. We had been very warry about taking vacations with just the two of us for a long time. It was incredibly challenging to find people trained to take care of Logan. The worry that something might go wrong while we were away always overshadowed our need to spend time together as a couple. We had taken a trip a few years before, and everything went fine, so we decided to roll the dice once again. Couples need their time together. Time for just the two of us was something we missed over the years. We had decided that this was the right time in our lives to begin doing that. We had arranged care for our kids, specifically Logan, and while still worried, we were ready to try and relax and soak in our little getaway. We had been in Cancun for only a day and a half when we got the call from my father.

Logan was running a severely high fever and visibly wasn't feeling well. We jumped into emergency mode and began making calls to Logan's doctors, which is not the easiest thing to do from Mexico. We spent the next four hours in panic mode, with the information that he would need admission to the hospital. We began making immediate flight plans back to the states and boarded a plane a few hours later. The next three hours became torturous, dealing with guilt for leaving him. My wife and I landed and raced to the hospital to be at his side and begin making provisions for his stay. Logan would be fine but would remain in the hospital for eight days.

Our life seemed to be going well up to that point. We had become accustomed to the challenges of our life. This incident changed us, though, as my wife and I struggled for years with forgiving ourselves for leaving. Not that we could have done anything differently being here, it was just the guilt that we weren't here. We had decided that we needed a getaway; we needed that time for just us. What we didn't realize is that it was our plan, what we felt was best. This incident reminded us that our assignment was to follow a different path in life, different from what we viewed as usual. We learned to appreciate our time together as a couple, no matter where or how long that was. Short conversations, a nice dinner out, or just a few minutes working together on the foundation or around the house became that much-needed couples time. Life can be fantastic if you let it; you can't force happiness. Happiness comes when you realize what's important and allow God to show you the glory that surrounds you each day. God gives us those moments with our spouse every day. Unfortunately, we had not learned to look for them until this moment and acknowledge them for what they were. In your relationship with your spouse, you often find the simplest treasures in moments we usually take for granted.

Logan spent a few more extended hospital stays for UTI's over the next few years, and we learned to adjust. He had become very involved in acting and performing in musicals through a group in our area called CYT, or Christian Youth Theater. Logan's schedule required him to perform in an upcoming series of shows when he spiked yet another fever the night before the first performance. Logan loves the theater, and this was his breaking point. He had never become agitated over any surgery, procedure, or hospital stay to this point, but this was now interfering with his greatest joy. Luckily, we established a relationship with many of his doctors over the years and explained the situation directly this time as they wanted to admit him once again. The doctor gave him the go-ahead to have an IV port installed to administer his antibiotics from home and so the show could go on. It has always amazed me how resilient Logan has been throughout his life. He makes his way through his struggles with ease. While the IV port would give him more flexibility, Logan was still feeling incredibly ill with the UTI infection. Most would consider this a significant obstacle; Logan viewed it as a minor inconvenience as he gave his all through each show. Thankfully, this was one of his last UTI infections for a while, as we discovered a new type of catheter that provided more sterilization. We know it may not be his last one, but we remain thankful that we have been given some relief from this for the time being.

Logan had experienced two surgeries shortly after birth but was far from done. Soon after concluding Challenger baseball's first year, we found out that he would need tethered cord surgery. Usually, the spinal cord floats around freely in the spinal canal. Still, because of scar tissue from the previous surgeries, the spinal cord begins to stretch as the person grows, permanently injuring the spinal nerves. This surgery would be to remove the scar tissue and allow the spinal cord to float as normal. We arranged to have the surgery over the summer months to eliminate the time missed from school.

The surgery day arrived, and Logan went into his procedure, as we began the long and agonizing wait for this to be behind us. The waiting and not knowing what is happening is the most harrowing experience for parents. Time seems to slow its pace, and your anxiety levels increase with each minute that goes by; there is almost nothing you can do to calm yourself. Before surgery, they give you an approximate time for the procedure, so you rely on that. The approximate time for this procedure was two hours, but as the minutes clicked away, increasing to the three-hour mark, our stress level and fear began to peak. Finally, a nurse asks you to come into a private room awaiting the doctor's visit, which you assume will be only a few minutes away. Never assume time when it comes to surgeons. They seem to have a timetable all their own, and a few minutes quickly becomes another agonizing lengthy wait.

I am so thankful for medical advances and the knowledge and expertise that doctors, particularly surgeons, possess. When they finally arrive to give you a report, you only want to know if your son is ok. Surgeons believe otherwise and explain the entire procedure in words above the limits of people not skilled in the medical profession. I know that day, I lost all patience as the surgeon continued to describe everything. I blurted out in a booming voice, "Is my son alive? Is he ok?" I think the surgeon may have realized our anxiety at that moment. She quickly reassured us that everything had gone according to plan, and he was doing fine. As a parent, I can skip the steps of the procedure. I need to know my son is ok. Unfortunately, sometimes doctors can get caught up in what they do and not what you might be feeling at the moment.

Logan would again have another tethered cord surgery about five years later, this one lasting longer than the first. Recovery time for both was lengthy, spending some time in the hospital and lots of time on his stomach to allow the area to heal. His final surgery to this point was a shunt revision to allow additional room for his shunt to continue to grow with him. Even as careful as we were to attempt surgeries over summer breaks, he still missed a good portion of his school, which caused further regression in his academics. The waiting and anxiety never improved with each procedure. The worry over what would happen next has never gone away; however, the expectation that it will come has become conditioned. Through all the surgeries, procedures, therapies, and delays, I have marveled at how Logan has accepted them and embraced who he is. He has never shown discouragement; he has never looked at himself as any less than anyone else. Logan has always approached life with joy and confidence.

The setbacks we have encountered over time are again unique to our situation. It would be easy to become depressed and question why. It would be easy to give up hope, to dwell on the negatives surrounding Logan. I feel blessed that God has given us this journey with him, to marvel at what he has overcome in such a short lifetime. I feel thankful for the medical advances that allow him so many opportunities that others in past situations like his were never able to receive. My wife and I have met so many other families with children with various disabilities. We see constant reminders of how bad things could be. All my children are gifts from God. Logan was just that gift that you get where the furnished instructions were in another language. Setbacks happen to everyone in life; it's what we do with them that helps us grow in wisdom and become stronger. Setbacks are only brief obstacles that God places in our path to remind us how to look for the joy and happiness surrounding us daily. Those small meaningful moments that we tend to overlook because of how busy our lives become.

CHAPTER 11

THE WORLD SERIES

"Impossible is just a big word thrown around by small
men who find it easier to live in the world they've been
given than to explore the power they have to change
it. Impossible is not a fact. It's an opinion. Impossible
is not a declaration. It's a dare. Impossible is potential.
Impossible is temporary. Impossible is nothing."

~ Unknown

Our foundation was growing in programs and the numbers of
families we reached in our local and surrounding areas. We had
expanded some of the programs we offered or promoted to include
basketball, dancing, and a small cheerleading team. More and more
people began to reach out to us to get their children involved. There was
still very little offered, and we provided the opportunities for something
year-round. Some families began traveling as far as forty to fifty miles to
have something for their child to do. Some families involved themselves
in every program we offered, and some only one or two as now they
had choices. It was an exciting time in the Lafayette area. Our biggest
problem was the number of ideas we had and just not having the time
to do it all. We ran everything out of our house and vehicles, which was
difficult, but we made it work.

While we seemed to be moving in the right direction, we still faced
several obstacles. To begin new programs, we needed space, somewhere

to offer these activities. The need for space meant we had to find businesses or organizations that would allow us to use their facilities. We needed insurance to protect ourselves, the facilities, and our participants. We discovered early on; this was not the easiest task. We had only our desire for our son and children like him to have things to do. We had only our faith that God would help us make this a reality. Once we found the right facilities, the next issue was promoting the programs. To this point, all we had was word of mouth. We had built a small network of participants but increasing our visibility to other families in our area became difficult. All businesses face growing pains in the first few years of existence, and we understood that. While we were a non-profit, we still expected the same struggles for our foundation. We had to practice patience and focus, knowing that it would come. In the book of Judges,18:6 tells us that, "The journey on which you go is under the eye of the Lord." God had set us on this journey, and we just had to put our complete trust in him, knowing that we would get there.

While we were thrilled with what we had accomplished to this point, we still knew we could do more. We both felt as if we were hitting a wall and couldn't move forward. We thought that we needed something to help build excitement; we needed a push. We knew the foundation had been God's plan for us all along, so we left it in his hands, only praying for guidance as to what was next. During our second season of basketball in early 2011, the next significant opportunity presented itself. Challenger's baseball coach pulled us to the side and gave us fantastic news. Lafayette's Challenger division received an invitation to play an exhibition game at this year's Little League World Series. There were almost 900 Challenger teams worldwide, and we were selected as one of two to represent the division! The Little League World Series was going into its 65th year of existence and featured teams from across the world each year. Many of the players in the past had become professional baseball players. Our kids now had an opportunity like no other. Now our players would have the chance to play on the same field of dreams, under the lights, in front of a national audience. The only challenge would be to get there.

When a little league team qualifies for the world series, they have limited time to fundraise. Still, besides travel, most of the qualifying team's costs are taken care of while in Williamsport, PA. It's a little different for the Challenger division. Travel is the first issue; as most of our kids could not handle a lengthy bus ride, we would need to fly. Flights would have to be arranged for families and a buddy to help with each participant on the field. Families would also need to take care of hotel expenses and transportation from the closest airport in Philadelphia, PA. A vast undertaking, but our advantage was something that qualifying teams didn't have; we had time to raise the money. The invitation gave us our first real glimpse of fundraising difficulties, especially for something for our population. The advantage we had was that this was big. The little league world series is well known; this was national pride.

We would be playing Baugo Little League Challenger division out of Indiana, which provided instant smack talk. The New Orleans Saints had just come off their first Super Bowl win in franchise history against the Indianapolis Colts. Of course, we began to send playful messages back and forth to Baugo, calling this round two. We were able to talk with those in charge of the Baugo team several times before the trip and began to build a common bond and understanding of their program and their area. The game wasn't about winning; we both had already won. The contest wasn't about competition; this was about our players having the opportunity of a lifetime. Excitement filled our area as billboards featured our kids, local news began showcasing our team, and word spread. Just weeks before we were to depart, the local little league team also qualified to play. Lafayette would now be sending two teams, only fueling the fire for more media coverage.

The day finally arrived when we would depart on our long journey. The fifteen members of our team, families, and buddies left out in the early hours of the morning with a big sendoff from Lafayette Little League park. Traveling with this large amount of people was a challenge. We made sure to arrive hours early to secure tickets, get everyone through inspection, and arrive at our flight area. We traveled most of the day by plane and landed in Philadelphia, PA, shortly after 9:30 pm. After securing our bags and rental vehicles, we departed for Williamsport, PA, attempting navigation through Philadelphia. These were the days when GPS was still relatively new, so we relied on printed maps and the lead vehicle for navigation. Williamsport, PA is still three hours from Philadelphia, so we knew we would arrive late that evening. What we didn't account for presented additional issues. First, the Philadelphia Eagles were playing a preseason game. By the time we secured our transportation to make our drive, the game had ended, releasing countless vehicles upon the roads. Once we left the city, the highways were not well lit, and a thick fog began to roll in, which further slowed travel. After driving for a considerable amount of time, we noticed the lead vehicle turning into a rest area, followed by our crew's remaining cars. We had missed our turn and now needed to circle back, adding another forty-five minutes to the journey. Sometimes God seems to throw further obstacles in front of you before giving you his gift; this just makes you appreciate it so much more.

We finally arrived just before three in the morning at our hotel. After checking everyone in, we retired to get some much-needed rest. I will not lie, everyone was a little cranky, but we knew it would be worth it. The next day was spent with sightseeing, parades, and visits to the little league museum, ending the evening with a large outdoor celebration and bar-b-que with both teams. Our moment was almost here, and you could feel the enthusiasm in each of the players. Meeting the team members and coaches from Indiana gave us a new outlook on what was happening in other parts of the country for our children. Who could've imagined how much this exhibition game meant to both of our communities? We retired early in anticipation of the next day; it was finally here.

The two teams arrived early for the game, taking in the World Series complex's sights and sounds. Each team entered the field to warm up along with their buddies as the stands filled with spectators. ESPN had set up a table and would be delivering a live telecast of the game. Signs adorned the stands cheering on each of the players while opening ceremonies commenced. The moment arrived with the umpire's shout of "Play Ball," and Lafayette went to bat first. Each smack of the ball exhilarated the crowd filling the stands with cheers for our children.

The Japanese team, who would eventually finish as runner up that year, hung over the fence in a show of heartfelt sportsmanship, shouting out words of encouragement to our kids with each play. Logan eventually had his turn at bat; his big sister Monique helped him to the plate and stood back. As Logan came to the plate, one of my most cherished moments was looking up and seeing the Goodyear blimp circling overhead. How many parents get to say that? Seconds later, Logan smacked the ball, and he and Monique raced down to first base, safe! I still remember the tears streaming out of my eyes as I watched him and the other players bask in their moment. Just a few years before, I had struggled with Logan's question of when he would get to play, and now, he was on center stage in front of the entire world. The game, of course, ended in a tie, but a win for everyone.

As we attempted to celebrate, we began to receive disheartening news. Hurricane Irene had formed along the east coast and was now heading for Philadelphia. We began to scramble, attempting to get through to the airlines to find out about our flights, which, of course, would be delayed. Most of the eastern coast began to shut down, anticipating the storm, which left us in limbo awaiting travel news. I and a few of the buddies, including Monique, had added problems. They were all in college, and their classes would begin on Monday; it was Saturday. I was about to commence student teaching, which also started on Monday. I had called to explain my dilemma but received a not so caring response from my new supervising teacher; I needed to be there Monday morning. We quickly decided to take one of the rental cars and make a cross country trip to Atlanta to meet our scheduled adjoining flight. Or, if needed, continue to travel by car back to Lafayette. The good news was a race to Atlanta meant that driving through the night should get us there with enough time; the bad news was that we still had another eight hours of driving ahead of us if we didn't make it. The situation wasn't favorable, but we felt it was our best move. We left out of Williamsport around nine pm Saturday evening.

Our mad dash towards Atlanta began as any other trip, relatively smooth. We all talked for hours about the experiences we had just shared, but talk quickly became sleep for my three passengers, which left me to navigate through the night and the mountains. Knowing that at some point, I would need to talk to the airline to explain the situation and arrange for us to board the connecting flight, I began attempting phone contact. My attempts proved pointless for hours as I could gain little reception through the mountains, but finally, around four that morning, I got through. I spoke as calmly as possible to the agent, explaining what we needed to do, and all seemed to be an easy fix. She asked to put me on hold while she finalized everything with our tickets, and moments later, I lost contact. Now fear began to creep in as I could only think of how exhausted I was and how I would make another eight hours if this hadn't been successful. I tried frantically to get back in touch with the agent, but the mountain terrain would not allow this to happen. I could only hope and pray that God would see me through this.

We rolled into Atlanta's international airport with a little over an hour to spare before our flight. We found the rental office and began attempts at returning the vehicle. We didn't realize that we also needed to call them before leaving Pennsylvania. The car needed to come back to the Philadelphia airport drop off. After several agonizing minutes, I agreed to pay a fine to drop off the vehicle and quickly raced inside to see if we had tickets. Moments later, I received the news that yes, indeed, everything had gone through, and we would be allowed to board. God guided our path on that journey and provided me the first relief I'd felt in over twelve hours. We boarded the plane, made our way back to Lafayette, and finally home. I've never felt so exhausted in my life, but now I could rest and prepare for my first day of student teaching. I contacted my wife, and she told me they were okay, but flights home would require another day of delay. All had worked out, just not how I had imagined it would.

God gives us so many moments in our lives to reflect on and from which to learn. Looking back at the world series's whirlwind experience demonstrated to me how hard you must sometimes work to achieve what God has in place for you. It's not always easy; if it were, we would take it for granted as we do with so many other things. Sometimes the obstacles in the path seem impossible. Still, in the end, through perseverance, the reward is always more than expected. We had all worked hard for that short moment in our children's lives. We created a moment that would not soon be forgotten by any of us, a juncture that helped to make our efforts in our community more noticeable. My wife and I will be eternally grateful to Lafayette Little League for two reasons. First, for allowing us the opportunity to start the Challenger division and give my son his answer. Second, for taking it a step farther and providing a once in a lifetime experience for our kids. After the world series Logan came in to talk with us; he wanted to let us know that he finished with baseball; he was retiring from the game. He had his sights set on something new.

CHAPTER 12

EVOLUTION

"It's not the strongest of the species that
survives, nor the most intelligent, but
the one most responsive to change."

~ Charles Darwin

Our foundation had grown slowly over the first three years, as we learned the ins and outs of self-promoting, fundraising, and further development of our network. Our house became a makeshift storage facility for equipment, shirts, and paperwork. We had developed our logo and an online presence but continued to struggle to bring awareness to our community. The existing programs we offered or promoted continued to do well but saw small growth with new participants. While we had accomplished one piece of the puzzle, making sure that there was something offered for our kids year-round, we never felt it was enough. Yes, they now had activities and programs to choose from and now had outlets throughout the year, but it was still only a few, and we wanted them to have more. Our biggest problem was that you could only do so much by yourself; there comes the point when you need help to move forward. Once we realized this and changed our focus, the foundation began to grow.

How did we go about additional help? Well, it began to fall into place through face-to-face contact with our parents. We both made sure to network as much as possible through every activity, really getting to know the parents, family members, and the child as much as possible. Eventually, some of the parents began calling us and began to ask if we would consider offering different programs. Of course, we wanted to grow; our only concern was time; we were only two people. God always knows how much you can handle, and to our surprise, most of those requesting new programs already had someone in mind to teach. The activities we offered quickly began to grow, offering more choices. Parents and volunteer teachers began to run the programs. While we wanted to be at everything, we had a bit of freedom in those times we couldn't.

Through getting to know our parents and families, we began to learn more about other disabilities. We had experienced frustration but now realized that the other families and organizations in our community needed to know we honestly had their best interest at heart. That wasn't going to happen just by establishing things to do for their kids. Through their kids, we had to develop programs through their needs, grow, and give them the choices they deserved. These parents quickly began to provide us with new ideas for programs that would benefit their children. They began to advocate with other parents of children with similar disabilities.

In just a few months, we established new programs such as yoga, music therapy, and art, suggested for our children with sensory and socialization issues. These programs presented a smaller and more relaxed environment for the kids to engage in addressing those limitations. Do it yourself, and gardening classes began shortly afterward, which provided our hands-on learners with an outlet. Photography and creative writing classes began to challenge participants with a flair for creativity. Our small cheerleading program thrived and began performing in front of audiences at half-times of football and basketball games for the University of Louisiana at Lafayette. The existing programs that we ran or promoted began to flourish by establishing new activities and additional energy and excitement as the number of families we reached began to grow. After changing our focus to explore the obvious, we had almost tripled in the number of families we worked with in just a few short years. We now had real year-round choices for our kids, and we had become an established visible resource with our community.

It has always amazed me at how fast things began to happen once we began to ask for assistance. We didn't have all the right ideas; we didn't have an overabundance of time. We just had the desire to create something for our kids in our community. We didn't realize that other parents wanted the same thing, but everyone gives what they feel they can. That's what we needed, what they could bring to the table no matter how big or small that help was. Almost overnight, we began to see a core group of parents involved in many of our activities that wanted to help. That help became an invaluable asset to our foundation and its growth.

We also gained an introduction to a young man who was a personal trainer and worked for a local gym through this core. He agreed to begin offering an adaptive fitness class for individuals with special needs in our community. God truly has a fascinating way of laying the groundwork for his path. Over a few years, the program began to do very well. One of the participant's caregivers became acquainted with him, which resulted in a budding relationship. That relationship developed over the years, and the two, as a result, were married. The fitness program continued to grow, and as a result, he decided to create a business called Unique Fitness. We don't take the credit for what happened; we only smile from ear to ear, knowing that we became a big part of his new life in a small way. A new life we discovered through an introduction and the guidance of God.

Logan had developed a new focus, something that would eventually open another door for our foundation. Logan had retired from the game of baseball. Why not go out on top? He had just finished a three-year run with the sport culminating with his last game at the Little League World Series. He wanted something else; we just didn't know what that was. My wife had heard of a musical Godspell being performed in town and by a new Christian Youth Theater organization. She and Logan decided to go and see the performance. That performance changed Logan's life immediately; he fell in love with it. I remember my wife telling me that as soon as the musical was over, that he looked at her and said, "This is what I want to do!" They met the man in charge after the show and asked for more information about the program.

CYT is a non-denominational non-profit organization nationwide designed to allow children to learn about theater after school and develop the skills necessary to perform. Performing for an audience perked Logan's attention; CYT was going to be his big new stage. Logan began enrolling in classes and tried out for the next show, he earned a small part, but you would have thought he had the leading role. He practiced regularly, and when the musical began a few months later, you could feel his joy as he rolled out on stage. We knew he had found his something, what he was genuinely interested in doing. Not by trying the things we established for him, but through his own eyes, through his feelings. Logan continued with CYT for years, performing in every musical that he could. He had found something he truly loved, and that passion worked in his favor in other areas of his life.

A few months before entering high school, he decided to talk with his counselor about getting into the gifted and talented theater program. Over the years, we've learned never to think the impossible, never to doubt. Performing was something he wanted, and if it meant God's plan for him would be further opportunities, it would happen. We applied for the program for him, and he gained an audition. We didn't know what would happen; we just prayed that God would allow him to understand if he didn't get in. We prepared ourselves for the negative because we didn't know that he would not fail. Shortly after his audition, Logan received a letter from the school board informing him of his acceptance into the gifted and talented theater program. He had found what he loved; Logan had worked hard for something he wanted and had found his path.

While we marveled over what Logan had accomplished through his desire to perform, we knew that he was unique. Not all children possess the ability to express themselves in the same way. The happiness and joy that we saw through Logan might be something that other kids with limitations might also enjoy but may never have or had the opportunity to explore. We decided to approach CYT and ask if we could offer a program through their organization, specifically designed around kids with disabilities. We wanted to present that opportunity to them, just to see if there was interest. Initially, we felt the hesitation we see when we talk with those who are not familiar with disability. Once we reassured them that we would run the classes and showcase performance, they decided to give it a try. Dreams theater classes began a few months later, offered over three ten-week sessions each year. Each session ended with a short showcase production on stage in front of a live audience. We held a lot of fear that it wouldn't work, but to our surprise, we watched as children came out of their shells and excelled. Through just a few introductions and Logan's determination, another program emerged.

A big hole missing in our area was a summer camp devoted to individuals with disabilities; some existed a few hours away, but we wanted something local. We talked about it for years, but the obstacles in putting one together seemed impossible to overcome. A summer camp would require many volunteer staff-hours to help create the perfect environment for an entire week. Of course, we would need facilities in which we could host the camp, and as we had found over the years, space was the most challenging portion of the equation. Could we provide enough activities that would keep the kids occupied and interested throughout the camp? Of course, the overall cost was also a significant consideration. Through Logan's journey with CYT, we met several people that became the contacts needed to make this happen. The local church hosting CYT's classes had the perfect facilities, with plenty of separate classroom spaces to break campers into smaller groups. We approached them with the idea and received the blessing of their willingness to use their accommodations.

God again had opened the door for us; now it was up to us to make this a reality. We immediately began planning, establishing a budget, and gathering volunteers for the week of camp. To our surprise, the church allowing us space also offered their housekeeping services to help with clean-up each day. Several of their pastors and ministers within the church offered to help with praise and worship each morning. That first year we set up Camp Unique for only the morning hours for the entire week. Late July in south Louisiana provides sweltering heat that would create obstacles in outdoor activities, so we figured cooler morning hours would help.

Camp Unique began that year with about forty participants of all ages and disabilities. It was a huge learning curve for us as an organization. As much as we planned, nothing could have prepared us for the stumbling blocks we hit that week. Through all of it, though, every camper wore a smile from ear to ear each day. We ended the week exhausted but filled with joy and happiness. God knew what we could handle that first year, but he also knew the camp would grow rather quickly. Those initial problems we encountered were nothing more than lessons for the future. The feedback we gained from each family made our summer camp something eagerly anticipated for years to come.

It still shocks me to this day, all that we accomplished in such a short time. The evolution of an idea to find something for my son to participate in and then becoming an organization that assists hundreds of individuals within our community has been truly astounding. It has come through hard work, desire, and faith in God. In the gospel of John 6:12, when Jesus completed his miracle of feeding the five thousand with just two fish and five loaves of bread, there is an abundance of crumbs leftover. He asks his disciples to "Gather up the fragments left over so that nothing may be lost." Jesus is giving us a simple message to notice the disregarded, which most view as worthless. To me, this is our journey, helping those that have gone unnoticed, paying attention, and becoming their voice. There have been times when my wife and I just wanted to give up because of frustration. It has become much more than we could have imagined. While I can sit back and marvel over what we achieved to this point, I realize we have only begun the journey. I know God has many more adventures in store for the foundation and our community. I can't wait to see what happens next.

CHAPTER 13

THE UNEXPECTED GIFT

"If I have seen further than others, it is by standing upon the shoulders of giants."

~ Isaac Newton

One of the most horrible experiences of my life was my time spent in math class. I love math, but in high school, I just wasn't an outstanding student. I remember the teacher going over the lesson of the day and assigning homework. I remember arriving home and sitting down to do my homework and feeling lost; One is just going to remember so much from a one-hour lesson. I didn't have anyone to rely on for help, only my book and how it described the process of going through the equations. I'd struggle through it and arrive at class the next day, knowing that my anxiety levels were about to peak. I would assuredly be called up in front of the class to work out a board problem. That's where anything I thought I'd learned went right out the window. I could feel the rest of the student's eyes watching every mark on the board. I knew the smart ones who got it were sitting back, laughing at me, and rolling their eyes. The teacher always seemed to jump in when it became apparent; I had no idea what I was doing. I could feel my teacher's frustration with me, making comments like, "we went over this yesterday" or "did you do your homework?" Yes, I'd done my homework; it just hadn't sunk in. I'm not getting it at this point. Those problems were intimidating to me; being put on the spot in front of the entire class with limited understanding forced me to undergo a series of uncomfortable feelings each day.

When you become a parent, particularly of a child with special needs, you begin to encounter similar feelings as if you were back in that high school math class. You might get lucky and find a few people that can share some insight with you in a conversation. However, the question that looms is how much retention of that information will my child have in just a few classroom discussions? You can read countless books devoted to the disability, which can offer some basic understanding, but every disability is unique. While you might find some similarities, there are so many undiscussed problems that you will encounter along your journey that you just won't find in a book. Advice from more experienced parents begins to sound like that teacher from years ago asking if you'd done your homework. You begin to feel stuck in a rut that you can't seem to get out of, no matter what you do. The future becomes terrifying, and at certain times you lose hope.

My wife and I discussed over the years that parents of children with disabilities seem to go through a series of stages of emotion. There is no time frame for going through these stages, as many parents seem capable of going through them quickly, while some seem to linger in certain areas. There is no graduation level; you may experience and pass a stage, and years later, find yourself right back in the same place. There is no formula for making your way through each step; you just have to go through it and hopefully find a way to make it out once again successfully. The first stage in this journey is grief. Your struggle with heartache over your child's diagnosis. The realization of how hard this journey will be not only on your child but also on you. The hopelessness of knowing something is wrong with your child, but you can't fix it. Grief begins at the moment of diagnosis, whether this is at birth or later in life. There is no timetable for your personal grief, and it is common to see one spouse move on while the other remains.

Once you pass the grief stage, you enter into the fear or anxiety step. Every parent worries about their child's future. I think this is natural. Still, parental fears become magnified, involving children with disabilities. Your mind races over possibilities from worry over your child being made fun of to the potential medical issues you may face down the road. Unfortunately, while in this step, you think of the worst possible scenarios. As you begin to get a grip on your fear, you move into a stage of anger. Now you seem to be mad at the world. Angry over your situation. You blame everyone and everything because you're convinced this is the reason your child has a disability. You blame the doctors, God, and even other family members, including pointing the finger at your spouse. Sadly, statistics show us that divorce rates in the United States are higher among couples who have a child with a disability.

The fourth stage involves isolation, either self-inflicted or an overwhelming feeling that friends and family have distanced themselves from you. You need someone to talk to, someone to share with, and help you make some sense of the situation. Regrettably, those people are trying to make sense of your plight in their way and are scared. They don't have the words you need, so they stay away, not wanting to upset your situation more. You also realize this and unconsciously distance yourself from them as well. You feel at this point that you have no one on which you can rely. Isolation can sometimes overlap the stage of failure or disappointment. You think that in some strange way, you've failed. You must have done something wrong for your child to have the problems they have. You begin to resent typical children's parents because of the overpowering feeling of disappointment that your child is not like their child. Feelings of failure can further mask themselves into extreme embarrassment. You feel that all eyes are on you when you are in public, almost as if they are judging you. These two phases can sometimes become a vicious circle, where one acts upon the other and does not allow you to progress.

Finally, you reach acceptance. You begin to accept the situation. You start to acknowledge that your child has so many gifts you've been overlooking while trapped within the previous phases. You begin to find the joy and blessing of your child. It's hard to admit going through these steps, these feelings, but I think it's important to recognize that we each go through them. It's part of our handling process. You can't help yourself if you don't know yourself. You can't help someone else unless you know and understand where they are in this process. All parents of children with disabilities go through this in one form or another. Some move through to acceptance very quickly, while some remain stuck in certain stages without the hope of moving forward.

Over the years of building our foundation, we focused on providing activities and programs for the children. We began to see children with all forms of disabilities come and participate. Our foundation was thriving, but along the way, we noticed something we hadn't expected. We began to see something change with our parents. Our kids were having fun while our parents gained the gift of a few minutes of ordinary. Time, they used to take a breath, to talk, to relax. My wife and I made our way through the stages of emotion. We had figured out how to deal with them, how to live life again. What we never realized to that point was that by accident, we had given these parents an outlet to do the same thing. A gift had been given to every parent, not by our intentions, but by circumstance.

Parents began to talk with other parents; friendships began to develop. Something extraordinary was happening right before our eyes. It didn't matter what their child's disability was; the stages of emotion each of us go through are the same. The activities became their opportunity to talk about each other's experiences and help each other through the various stages, without realizing what was happening. My wife and I do not take the credit for this; it happened on its own. People bond when they have things in common; it was only natural for these connections to occur. What we didn't realize at the time is that this was also happening for us. We were forming friendships with several families that began devoting time to volunteering with the foundation.

My wife and I decided to see if we could build upon this and scheduled a couple's night out. Just a night to have dinner, a few drinks, and relax. We didn't know if it would take off, simply because of the struggle that most of our parents go through to find someone to watch their kids. Each child has their own unique set of needs that you must address, which require skilled and trained caregivers. One of the couples we had become friends with over the years had recently taken an overnight getaway for their anniversary. They later divulged to us that it was the first time they had been away and alone on an overnight stay in over eighteen years! You can't just pick up the phone and call the fourteen-year-old girl with a babysitting service down the street. Parents must feel comfortable with who they leave their child with, and it only becomes more magnified when leaving your child with special needs. You must not only have someone trained; you must have someone you trust. Something very uncomplicated, such as a night out for typical parents, can become a complicated nightmare in the special needs community. It is not uncommon to see parents of children with special needs give up luxuries like this altogether.

Our first couple's night went better than expected, with nine couples attending. We had taken over a little side room in a local restaurant and moved around the room, talking and laughing with each person. Conversations ranged from light, funny stories to intensely complicated issues with doctors, schools, government agencies, and our children. It was therapeutic for everyone involved. We had known so many of these parents for years, but we instantly became close friends that one night. We finally had friends that we could share our concerns. We now had people who jumped for joy over our child's smallest accomplishment. We now had allies that could see things from our perspective and always provided an outlet for our emotions. God chose each of us to live a path that required a large amount of strength that required giving things up, which most typical parents take for granted. We did this daily with no expectations for ourselves, only to better our children's lives. The gospel of Matthew 10:39 says, "He who has found his life will lose it, and he who has lost his life for My sake will find it." We had all lost the life we thought we should have. God knew what we had given up and had given us the means to find a precious gift, a new life, the gift of community.

Leaving our parent's night out, we felt recharged. A new enthusiasm formed within our parents' group, and it showed quickly through our programs and activities. Those programs became not just something for our children to enjoy, but something we all looked forward to because it now meant catching up with our friends as well. Rough weeks became much simpler to manage now having an outlet. The foundation not only grew into what my wife and I had initially envisioned but now it had grown into a family. For the first time since we had begun, my wife and I now felt as if we had the support we would need to continue. It didn't seem as overwhelming as before; the path had become much clearer.

Our parent outings continued for months with a full range of topics discussed. One issue that began to take center stage was that our children were becoming adults. Typical parents see this happen as well. Their main concerns are for their child to get into an excellent college, maybe have a career in the military, and the hopes they will meet that special someone and get married. Our concerns were what will life be like after high school for our children? Most of our kids would never attend college, and none would have a military career opportunity. Our kids were becoming adults, and we needed to begin focusing on the future.

I think all children have the same three desires in life, no matter their abilities or inabilities. They want and need social companionship. They need friends, people to talk to and with whom they can enjoy life. They want a sense of purpose, something to be proud of answering the question of why am I here, what was I meant to do? They desire to leave the nest, have a place of their own to live, somewhere other than mom and dad's house to call home. For typical children, these three desires or needs generally take care of themselves naturally. They continue in school, build friendships there, find jobs after completing their education, and eventually move out. Our parent's group knew this was a different reality for our children. This concern now became a new direction that our foundation would take, one that we needed to happen yesterday.

CHAPTER 14

WHEN LIFE GIVES YOU LEMONS, ASK FOR A LIMO

"And when it rains on your parade,
look up rather than down.
Without the rain, there would be no rainbow."

~ **G.K. Chesterton**

The world of special education is challenging when students get to high school. Most parents want their child included as much as possible, but that still comes with limitations. Football games, parties, and school dances that most typical students enjoy are not necessarily accessible for students with disabilities. While the invitation is open to all, many students who already deal with daily challenges choose not to attend. Fear of the unknown is primarily the driving force behind this lack of participation. Parents are fearful that their children may be bullied or mistreated. Faculty and staff worry about school liabilities. The students have multiple concerns that make not going all the more attractive. Many students with disabilities miss these opportunities to appreciate their short time in the high school environment.

Logan never let any of that stop him. He made sure he lined up a date for every dance and was always very active in school functions. He would mention to us that many of his friends from his special needs classroom would never attend. We knew that it bothered him but would always reassure him that some people don't like to go to things like that in school. He always responded that they didn't know what they were missing. He was right.

Towards the end of Logan's sophomore year, he received a big surprise from one of his classmates. One morning, a young girl in his adapted physical education class came in with a decorated poster asking him to the Lafayette High school prom. Of course, he said yes! Logan came home that afternoon beaming; you could see the joy in his eyes. We knew then that this night meant the world to him. Why did it mean so much? Because he would get to spend the evening with many of his friends and share in their delight.

Logan decided that he needed to bring his date in style. Meaning he wanted a limousine to take him, his date, and several friends to the event. Logan was insistent. Over the years, we've learned that nothing will stop him when he makes up his mind to do something. My wife attempted to argue that it would be expensive, costing over five hundred dollars. His answer was simple; he would sell lemonade to raise enough to pay for it himself. How could you not laugh? My wife just looked at him and said, "really?" She began to remind him that he and his little brother Lucas had opened their lemonade stand about a year or two before this idea. They had spent many afternoons outside during the summer months peddling their lemonade, making a few bucks each week. I believe their best week totaled about forty dollars. He became a little agitated and stormed off, saying, "You don't know what you're talking about!"

We knew we would have to agree to his master plan but didn't want him to become discouraged. Once he calmed down, my wife talked with him a little more about it and offered to make him a sign to help drum up sales. He agreed, and a short while later, he came out with a smile from ear to ear to show me. The sign read, "Please buy some Lemonade, need a limo for my lady!" A catchy little slogan. You could tell he was pumped and ready to begin. We expected him to become discouraged after just a few days, with very little to show for it. We've never been so wrong in our lives.

What we didn't realize was that Logan was planning to get the word out in style. Over the years, he had built up many friends and contacts through Facebook. I came home from work on his first day out in front of our house to find him busy sending private messages and making posts. I remember smiling at how focused he was on making this happen and wished him good luck. Within a few hours, my wife arrived home and came inside to tell me that he'd raised almost three hundred dollars that afternoon. I was amazed! How was this possible? In one afternoon, he'd already made six times the amount he and his little brother had made after weeks of work last summer. What was different?

My wife and I laughed that night at how determined he was. Even with all the problems he had faced during his life, he still found a way. We figured he had raised about all that he would and decided to pay for the additional cost when he fell short. Again, we had no idea what was about to happen. The next day I arrived home to find Logan outside at his lemonade stand, continuing to work tirelessly on sending messages to his contacts. I went inside to start making dinner, and about thirty minutes later, my wife came through the door. It was unusual for her to be home so early in the day. She looked at me and said, "You're not going to believe this!" My mind began racing as to what could be happening as she began to explain.

Logan had sent messages to his entire contact list. Some of those contacts were people he had met over the years, working in local television, newspapers, and radio. These contacts began running his story throughout the day. My wife explained that two news crews were on their way over to interview him for that evening's newscast. A local radio host was championing his cause most of the day, and as a result, his business was booming! One of his customers had pulled up and handed him five hundred dollars and told him to have fun before driving away. The man will forever be a mystery as Logan didn't get his name. We walked outside in disbelief as we observed both news crews arrive to begin setting up for their interviews. My wife continued to explain that she had received a call that day from a trolley company offering the use of a trolley for 500 dollars. They usually charge 1500 dollars, but they had heard Logan's story and wanted to provide their services for the night at the same price as a typical limo.

We watched as Logan beamed with pride during his interviews, knowing that he would be on the news that evening. A steady flow of vehicles continued down our street, coming to support Logan and buy a glass of lemonade. It was an unreal moment. In two days, Logan had raised a little over 2,000 dollars and secured his ride with a modified price. Since Logan did not need the money, he decided to donate his earnings after paying for the trolley. He split the money three ways, between Christian Youth Theater, which had meant so much to him, the D.R.E.A.M.S. Foundation of Acadiana and the local radio host who had championed his cause. Logan told us that the radio host's daughter was fighting cancer, and he wanted to help with her medical expenses. Most young men his age would have selfishly spent the money on their enjoyment. Logan once again demonstrated his selflessness in his desire always to help others.

The night of the dance came and went, leaving so many smiling faces. Logan's friends spoke for weeks about their ride in the trolley. Logan accomplished his goal of creating a lasting memory for so many. A few weeks after the dance, my wife decided to enter Logan into a Lemonade day contest that is put on annually by Raising Cane's restaurant. We were both still in disbelief of what had just happened, and I think she wanted to let others know of his accomplishment. We were soon surprised to find out that he had been named entrepreneur of the year for the state of Louisiana. Corporate employees arrived at our home a few days later with the award and plenty of additional surprises. On top of the state award, Logan later received notification that he had finished second in the national contest. All of this from his desire to make a memorable night for his friends.

Logan has taught me more about overcoming obstacles than any other person in my life. He has never looked at himself as disabled. He has never let his wheelchair hold him back. Most of us tend to make our problems more significant than what they are. We worry and agonize over all the complications life throws at us. I look at how Logan handled a seemingly impossible task, with no worries, no stress. It shows me an entirely new view of the world we live in, a world through child-like eyes when everything is simple. I've spent every day since that moment trying to view the world as he does. My problems now seem fewer and far less complicated.

CHAPTER 15

ALL THE WORLD'S A STAGE

"All the world's a stage, and all the men and women merely players; They have their exits and their entrances; And one man in his time plays many parts, His acts being seven ages."

~ **William Shakespeare**

Our fears and concerns for Logan quickly became a reality in an extremely short time. Logan had made his way as best he could through high school. He had suffered setbacks through it all but always pushed forward and gave it everything he had. Over the years, Logan had fallen too far behind the typical academic pace to hope for achieving a high school diploma. When he would make strides in academics, he would suffer another setback. He would need to undergo a new surgery or experience another lengthy hospital stay, which would cause those strides to deteriorate. Each holiday or unforeseen time away from school would cause him to regress no matter what we attempted. He excelled in his theater classes but sadly made little strides in building upon basic subjects. He spent most of his days in high school, in and out of resource or special education classrooms that never seemed to push him hard enough. As a result, he approached graduation reading at about a fourth-grade level and solved math problems at a high third-grade level.

His strength was in his personality and listening comprehension, both of which complimented him well in the theater.

Logan had made his mark on his high school; he had indeed impacted the faculty and student body. The day's structure became very important to his life as we knew it would be one of the most challenging things to replace. He had fallen in love with all aspects of the theater, thriving with every performance. During high school, his performances multiplied. He now appeared in shows through school, the gifted and talented program, and Christian Youth Theater. He was always incredibly busy, there was never time for rest, and he loved every minute of it. This tremendous amount of time he spent with theater was a blessing and seemed a curse because we knew very soon it would end abruptly.

Logan ended his high school career with a bang. To our surprise, he had worked with his teachers through the gifted and talented program to develop, direct, and star in his finale, which was simply called the Logan show. Logan had spent hours upon hours finding just the right people to play minor roles, work out the transitions of three scenes, and finally direct his masterpiece. We arrived at the theater, not knowing what to expect as he had kept his lips sealed throughout the process. We only knew it would be noteworthy because, as he had told us, we would be amazed!

The show commenced with a scene from the Lion King musical; the circle of life African costumes and characters adorned the stage. Logan made his entrance as Rafiki chanting, "Ingonyama," and holding the baby Simba. The crowd of about one hundred people cheered with tears streaming down their faces as they witnessed his pure joy and love of being on stage. The show segued into scenes from the musicals Les Misérables and Seussical, complete with quick costume and set changes. He was at his finest moment. He was showcasing himself to the world, and not a person in the theater that night looked at him as someone with limitations. They looked at him as a talented performer.

The show ended with a complete outpouring of love. Each of the performers taking the time to address Logan and explain the impact he had made in their lives over the years in high school. As a parent, we only wanted to see Logan succeed, but hearing the impressions that Logan had made on these students and teachers was a precious gift. They had learned to look beyond the wheelchair. They had learned that there was so much more to him than his shortcomings. They saw Logan as we saw him, someone special, someone who could change lives. The night concluded with his gifted teacher asking him to become her assistant director in her upcoming shows. She recognized his talent; of course, he said yes. His life in the theater was far from done. It had become part of him and a part of us; the show must go on. That night I completely understood why God had created our son the way he did.

The day of Logan's graduation arrived. He would not graduate with a typical high school diploma. He received a certificate of completion, which is standard for students in the special-education realm who can not meet the specific diploma requirements. He did have the opportunity to go back and continue in school for another two years because of special-education laws. Unfortunately, that time would only include academics; there would be no more theater. His academic progress had come to a standstill over the past five to six years. It made little sense to continue, especially taking away the thing he truly enjoyed. We decided Logan should tell us what he wanted, and after explaining his options, he told us he wanted to move on. He'd had enough of high school. We knew the future would be a rough ride. Still, without seeing any further preparation from his High school to transition to the real world, we had to agree with him. We realized that it would be next to impossible for him to catch up to grade level pace and achieve the requirements for a traditional diploma in just two years. We would only be prolonging the inevitable.

Logan's graduation ceremony commenced, and he rolled in with over 400 classmates. He was excited, a big part of his life was coming to an end, and he couldn't wait for the next adventure. He had become an enormous part of his high school as most of the students knew and loved him, as well as the faculty and staff. His moment arrived as he rolled up onto the stage and upon hearing his name, a thunderous roar of cheers came over the crowd of thousands in attendance. Since his birth, I had always worried about how he would do in school. I worried about bullies, about potential failure, about him getting hurt. I know every parent goes through something like this with each child; you just hope and pray they find their place. Upon hearing his name called and watching him move to receive his certificate, I became overpowered with emotion. I felt excitement for him, a sense of fear, and a sense of relief.

The next few weeks went by relatively easy as Logan now adjusted to summer. However, it doesn't take him long to become bored with a relaxed environment. He's a people person and needed that human contact. We attempted to keep him busy and entertained, but he was at a point where he needed his friends; it just wasn't the same with mom and dad and the rest of the family. Luckily, my wife had built her CPA practice over the years and worked with several local clients that she felt might present some opportunities for him. One of those, a local restaurant, decided to give Logan a chance at a job. Working at a restaurant was right up his alley. He would have something to do, plenty of people to visit with, something with a little structure to his week. Logan's interview resulted in his immediate hire starting the next week as a host. You would've thought he had landed his dream position with the thrill in his voice as he told everyone he had a job. Logan began work and initially encountered a few obstacles but overcame them quickly. While the job was only two nights per week, it seemed to give him that outlet he needed, at least for the time being.

For months Logan seemed occupied, but there was still a definite absence of theater in his life. He began to assist directing with his former gifted teacher in a future production, which gave him an outlet. Still, it was different; it just wasn't enough to fill the void. Moving from something that had been such a big part of his life to now, something with limits just wasn't working. He needed a challenge; he needed his next big adventure. Soon after completing his production, he came and told us he wanted to go to college. That sickening feeling I'd had years before when he'd asked me when he was going to get to play rushed right back in.

Finding and establishing programs and activities seemed so simple now; this was something I didn't think could be accomplished.

Logan didn't have a high school diploma. He was behind the norm academically; this didn't seem like a possibility. We tried to explain in the best way we could, but Logan had made up his mind. So, I asked what any parent would ask, "What do you want to go to college for?" I figured he just wanted to go because all his friends from high school went, and he wanted the same experience, I was wrong. He had done his homework; he wanted to go to culinary school and become a chef. My wife and I have never told him he couldn't do something; that was something he'd have to learn independently. We felt sure there was no way but decided to support him in finding out. We set up a consultation at the local community college a few weeks later. If it weren't a possibility, she would be the one to tell him.

To our surprise, trade school functions a little differently than college. Primarily, you don't need a high school diploma or entrance exams to become a student. All that was required was an application to the school and a few forms of ID. Once again, God had presented us with what we saw as an impossible task, only to show us that nothing is impossible. Over the next two months, Logan gained acceptance into culinary school, purchased his books and the equipment he needed, and met with the person in charge of accommodations. We hired a person to help him through his day with notetaking and maneuvering around campus. Logan attending college was becoming a reality. My anxiety levels peaked once again, knowing this wouldn't be easy by any means. There would be a considerable amount of reading, which I knew I could do with him. It would just be time-consuming, not to mention that some of his equipment included knives. One was a big eight-inch blade! I feared he wouldn't do well, but I feared him cutting off a finger even more.

Logan began classes with excitement in his eyes. He couldn't wait to learn about cooking and baking. Confirmation of my reading fears and his assignments came very soon after his classes began. I sometimes spent three or more hours a night helping him through it. He excelled at the class's hands-on portions. Though he had difficulties using the knives, he soon learned proper usage and technique. If only he could've learned everything hands-on. He soon encountered testing, which, even with the accommodations given, were overwhelming for him, specifically the culinary math, which involved measurements. I worked hours upon hours with him at home; he just couldn't get it. I think he could have eventually over time, but unfortunately, the curriculum didn't allow for that time. He made his way through the semester with his frustration building, he was in over his head with the math, and he knew it. The semester ended with him achieving all passing grades except for that math class. It was a point of reflection for Logan. He had struggled through something like he had never encountered before. There were points where he saw success, primarily through the hands-on lessons; there, he excelled, although he did suffer one deep cut on a finger at one point. It was the academic side that worked against him. He had met one of his limitations head-on with no fear, only with reminders that he did have limits. He ended that semester and came home, and that night he told us, "I made a twenty percent on my test, and I cut my finger; I'm done with college." We all face challenges within our lives that create resistance; it's what we do with those challenges that shape us. Logan had met one of his and struggled. He had become stronger for it, and he had learned an important lesson. God sometimes has a different plan.

CHAPTER 16

DREAMS MANUFACTURING

"Some people dream of success, while other people get up every morning and make it happen."

~ **Wayne Huizenga**

A new problem was beginning to surface through several of our families. Their children were now becoming adults and exiting school. Exiting high school for these families was beginning to cause problems within their households since parents still needed to work. The disruption to the structure of their child's day caused issues. Families now had to find other means of caregivers for the children. Without that structure in their day, the children were regressing, and some were slipping into depression. We had personally encountered these problems with Logan recently. We were still working through it and adjusting and struggled to find answers. Most of our kids didn't have the means or opportunities to attend college, nor did they possess the skills needed to find and maintain gainful employment. As a parent, you see this day coming but seem to convince yourself that it will work itself out. It doesn't, and you now wake up to a new and complicated reality.

This undeniable situation began to open the doors for frantic discussion between our parents and what we would do now. There was no quick fix to the problem. In our community, there are a few day programs available. Each existing program still has limits of capacity, and some parents just weren't sure if that was the right place for their child. Some government agencies offered job shadowing and placement, but with limits and with no guarantees. Many of our dual-income households began to readjust work schedules, sometimes taking significant pay cuts, so that there would be a parent available during the day. Single parent homes did not have this option and relied heavily on family members for help. Even those few who were able to readjust and or find a day program still saw dramatic changes in their children.

None of us had the right answers; we only had each other and our ideas. My wife and I knew we had created a sense of community for these children and their parents over the years, but that wasn't enough. They needed something more as they got older; they needed a sense of purpose. It's tough to get up and get out of bed in the morning, especially if you don't have a reason. The transition from High school was a much larger problem than we had initially encountered years before. Establishing an activity was one thing, but providing the answer to what we do after high school was another. My wife and I knew we had an uphill battle in front of us with numerous obstacles, including transportation, job training and readiness, and jobs for our kids. We couldn't overcome these obstacles overnight, but we knew it had to happen; this was our next undertaking.

We met with our board of directors for our annual meeting to discuss the state of the foundation. We decided this would be the place to briefly describe the situations now arising for many of our families. Our board brainstormed, searching for ideas on how we could make an impact. One of our board members mentioned that they knew of a man that ran a meat pie business and was looking to retire. His family didn't want to continue running the company, and he might be open to us taking it over. Meat pies are pies filled with delicious meats, such as beef, pork, and turkey and are very popular in Louisiana. My wife and I looked at each other in astonishment; this might be an answer. We asked to set up a meeting to see the operation and discuss the possibilities with the owner.

A few weeks later, my wife put together a crew of parents and our kids to head up the road to take a test run of the facilities. Once again, we saw God put things into place right before us. The kids went to work in the meat pie factory. They each had the opportunity to place dough on small machines, fill the dough with seasoned meat, and use hand cranks to rotate and wrap the combination into pies. It was a simple process, but our kids loved it. My wife discussed the business aspects with the owner and left the factory that day filled with excitement; this had become a genuine possibility in just a few days. That evening my wife and I discussed the day in detail until the early hours of the morning. We knew this would be a considerable undertaking, but it needed to happen. She had worked out details to take the business and the 125-year-old recipe over and continue paying the man a percentage of sales for his retirement. The additional positive was that it was an existing business with existing orders; we would not start up from scratch; we could build upon established clientele. We would place the company under the umbrella of the foundation. The idea was not to institute the company for a significant turnaround; we wanted to create jobs for our kids. We would be okay breaking even, but all would go back into the foundation for future projects if we made money.

Over the next few months, we gained board approval to begin the Dreams Manufacturing company. We found space in the heart of Lafayette and started the renovations necessary to open the doors. We were fortunate to discover that one of our parents and her daughter would run the operation for us during the day. The business would require the right full-time people to work with our kids. Good things come with a price, as we quickly encountered the obstacles of opening a venture like this. All processing had to be strictly enforced by USDA guidelines, which required a USDA agent to be on-site for most of the day. Job, food, and supply costs had to be determined and monitored weekly. Packaging and dealing with several distributing companies presented its own set of problems, not to mention future sales and getting the word out to the public. These problems posed numerous hurdles and additional stress. Still, the drive to make this a reality for our kids outweighed the difficulties encountered.

I was teaching vocational and interviewing skills and knew that we needed this as part of the process. We established several questions for our kids seeking employment; we sent those to parents along with a simple application to fill out. The idea was to allow our kids to practice interviewing at home in a more relaxed environment before being asked to sit down on a one on one interview. Over the next few days, we hosted our annual summer camp and knew that most potential employees would be in attendance. We arranged for and set up a side room and arranged times for interviews during breaks and after the day was complete. The business was happening, and we wanted the hiring process to be as real as possible. After all of the interviews were complete, we decided to hire twenty-one individuals with disabilities to begin working in just a few short weeks. We were able to hire so many because most would only work one to two shifts per week, for three hours at a time. It doesn't sound like much, but for our kids, it was all they could handle.

We held our ribbon-cutting ceremony on December 7th, 2018, with all employees, families, and local area news crews in attendance. Our new employees beamed with pride as they were each interviewed and were able to say for the first time, "I have a job." Dreams Manufacturing opened its doors the next day with orders to fill for several large jail systems in the state. A few months after opening the doors, we acquired bulk orders for several nursing homes, a hospital system, and various bookstore locations on the University of Louisiana's campus at Lafayette. Our employees stayed busy and loved coming to work. On average, they were producing 15,000 plus meat pies per month for distribution. We were able to establish ourselves in twelve local grocery store locations to hit the smaller market. Dreams Manufacturing was up and running and growing.

The creation of Dreams Manufacturing has given us a tangible and visible presence within our local community. To this point, to be involved in Dreams meant that disability had somehow affected your life. For those not affected, well, they may have heard of our foundation, but that was as far as it went. Most people tend to involve themselves with charities and non-profits near and dear to their hearts. The meat pie business gave us a new advantage and helped us reach more of the public. If nothing else it demonstrates daily, these individuals are employable, which will hopefully lead to further job opportunities for each of them within our community.

We still had an extensive task in front of us, but we'd taken a step in the right direction. While we are so proud that we could employ twenty-one individuals with disabilities, we realize this is a tiny percentage of our area's disabled population. Our focus would continue, now with much more excitement and belief in what we were trying to accomplish. Creating jobs was only a piece of the puzzle. We also needed to figure out transportation concerns. We knew that even by opening other job possibilities, most of these individuals would require further job training and job readiness skills. The future for our population looks brighter each day, and we will continue to open new doors, one pie at a time.

CHAPTER 17

SIBLING DEVELOPMENT

"Siblings are the people we practice on,
the people that teach us about fairness
and cooperation and kindness and
caring – quite often the hard way."

~ Pamela Dugdale

One of the hardest parts of raising multiple children is devoting a proper amount of time to each of them. Each of them is special in their way and needs that attention from their parents. When you spend too much time with one, you leave the others feeling left out, which results in jealousy between siblings and a feeling of resentment towards the parents. I felt this firsthand growing up in a divorced home. I lived with my mother, so she was always around; I never had to share her attention with anyone.

On the other hand, my dad had remarried and had two daughters of his own, so my visits came with mixed emotions. I was always excited to see and spend time with him, but at the same time, I felt like the third wheel. I never truly felt like I was a part of his family; I was just that kid who came to visit during the summer or holidays. I was just there. It took me several years to understand and develop a relationship with my dad and my two half-sisters. My sisters had done nothing wrong; I had just refused to allow a connection to happen because of my jealousy towards them. My dad had only chosen the path of least resistance and had moved on with his life. It was easy for me to be angry with the situation, much more comfortable than finding forgiveness in my heart and moving forward.

While my mom was always around, I grew up watching her struggle with relationships with her siblings. They always seemed to be fighting about something. Their family's result was to write each other off; there was no working through the problem; we just no longer talked to them for a while. I missed seeing my uncles and my aunt but became used to this being the norm. I felt that this must be how all families were, and there wasn't much you could do about it. My frustration only increased with my view of how a family should operate and how I viewed my relationship with my dad and two sisters.

Once I began dating my wife and spending time with her family, I realized that a family took work, lots of work, especially with multiple siblings. My wife and her siblings would fight and still do, but the difference was they worked through it in a short amount of time. They never let anything destroy their bonds. The short time I had with my wife's parents showed me that each child needed that individual time with their parents; they needed that small reassurance of love. Time was only one factor, as forgiveness was the key to success. No matter what one of the kids did, my wife's parents were always there, always the family's rock.

Each one of us handles life differently, and there isn't a perfect model. I've always loved two verses from Philippians 2:3 – 4, which says, "Do nothing from selfishness or empty conceit, but with humility of mind regard one another as more important than yourselves; do not merely look out for your own interests, but also the interests of others." Not the easiest thing to do, notably when you are angry with someone. But if we can see the importance of someone, especially those we love, we have to place their feelings higher than our emotions and desire to show them, love. Sometimes this is the most difficult of crosses to bear. We naturally perceive that our feelings are more important and have difficulties understanding and letting go of those adverse feelings towards the other person involved.

I've never judged anyone based on their actions, and I never will. We all make mistakes and act foolishly at times. I've often wished things could have been different in my childhood. Through those struggles, I've realized that I developed personal bonds with each of them in my way over time. Those struggles taught me that this was not the way I wanted to raise our children. My wife and I had to be better; we had to look at our children's needs above our own, no matter the cost.

One of the first steps, I believe, was choosing to raise our children in the Catholic faith; this was simply our choice. I feel that a marriage should be unified, in everything, including your religious beliefs. Up to the point of our decision, I always felt like the tramp of Christianity. My baptism took place in the Lutheran church as a baby. My Grandparents on my dad's side took me to weekly services through the Methodist church until I was twelve. Then we moved. Later my only experiences with going to church were occasionally through my friends at various non-denominational churches or going to midnight mass with my Great Aunt.

My parents didn't go to church regularly, and I never really understood why. I loved being at church; it felt good. Oddly, I loved the mid-night mass with my great aunt the most, I had no idea what was going on because it was in Latin, but it was beautiful and would stick with me for days. My wife was raised Catholic and began bringing me to mass with her weekly once we started dating. As we got closer to marriage, it seemed to be an easy decision to convert to Catholicism.

God blessed us with three children, all of whom had different needs. Monique came into our family through non-traditional means. We knew she would face numerous difficulties growing up losing her biological parents. Monique was our first, so giving her all the attention in the world was not hard in the beginning. We did everything with her daily, she was our focus, and we let nothing get in the way of that spotlight within our lives. In hindsight, we probably spoiled her a bit, overcompensating for the loss she had already encountered. Still, we wanted to make sure Monique knew that we loved her. It was awkward at first attempting to explain to people who didn't realize the situation. Still, over time we realized it was only uncomfortable because we allowed it to be that way. She was every bit of our family; she was our little girl. Unfortunately, Monique was always the one I worried about the most. She had faced so much in her young life, losing both her parents and then gaining us and adjusting to her new family. Then the sudden issues and problems we would encounter with the birth of Logan. My wife and I just couldn't imagine how all this was affecting her; we just kept her in our focus as best we could through all of it.

Logan entered this world with a bang and never stopped. We immediately knew he would face several difficulties throughout his life. We realized the limits it would place on our attention to Monique. Every older brother or sister must go through this to some extent, but this was different, more magnified. Attempting to explain to a seven-year-old girl why things like this happen is incredibly tricky, especially when you don't understand yourself. Prayer became our only resource as we knew we had much more to think about than our son's immediate needs. God had blessed us with two beautiful children made in his image, not in the way most people assume they will welcome their children into the world. God had given us a responsibility like no other, knowing what we all could endure as a family. As parents, our job became simply following his direction, responding to his push to be better, to do more.

Monique responded better than we expected to the situation; she was so proud of her little brother. It was amazing to see how nurturing she was towards Logan, always playing with him and wanting to help in any way she could. I think Logan's complications may have created a diversion, a new focus for her in some ways. Our time we had both spent with her now became divided as one of us would have to work with Logan while the other gave attention to her. We made sure to trade-off as we planned each week. We knew that spending time with her on homework, playing in the backyard, or watching from the sidelines at soccer practice was essential. We couldn't overshadow that time and need because of the demands of time spent with Logan. God knew what he was doing; we were just following his plan. Monique grew up spending most of her time with Logan through the initial surgeries and complications. By the time he was ready to make his mark on the world, she was about to enter high school. She always amazed me at how she responded to every situation handed to her. While she did deal with some anxiety issues, her inner strength and faith in God would always overcome whatever life gave her.

My wife and I thought we were through with having children. God had given us one of each, a boy and a girl, and with the situations we had already encountered, we felt that this was all we could handle. I've always felt that God is a bit of a practical joker, and just when you think you've got things figured out, he hits you with the surprise! Our surprise came a little over seven years after Logan was born. My youngest child Lucas now entered the scene as a strong and healthy boy. The big difference in our lives was that we had created the foundation, and our time was spread very thin. Monique divulged to me years later that she felt some remorse about us having another child simply because of our incredibly busy schedule. She felt as if raising Lucas would somehow now become her responsibility. I had always thought that any resentment would have come from the time and attention we had to give to Logan; I had no idea she felt differently. Logan was over the moon with excitement about being a big brother and instantly began to bragging to all who would listen about his new title.

Lucas was all boy, always running and getting into trouble; he seemed never to stop. He had no choice when it came to our life with the foundation, and he became a part of it. He seemed to enjoy helping with all the kids in our programs, even at a very young age, but it was always apparent when he needed his time with us. Logan and Lucas played and fought as any two brothers would. Lucas, usually the instigator of most situations, would torment his brother. Still, Logan quickly found the means to stop the feuds by placing Lucas into a headlock. Logan would secretly talk Lucas into climbing cabinets to seek out candy or other sweets for the two of them until, of course, we found their hiding holes. Their time as young boys was just like any other home; later, as they got older, we began to see some separation in their relationship. That dissolution was not due to Logan's disability; it was due to their personalities, which again happens in most families. Monique would split her time with both boys, doing something special with each of them each week. She had already experienced adjusting time over the years, and I think it helped her to be able to do the same for them.

Nothing was ever perfect in our family. We just adjusted to the new plan as it happened and trusted in God. We had our fights and bad times just as any other family does, but we always made time for every family member somehow. I've asked both Lucas and Monique if they ever felt left out because of all that we did with our foundation, but both have always said no. Speaking as a parent of a child with a disability, you sometimes feel guilty about all the time you spend with them. Unfortunately, a great deal of that time is spent primarily in doctor's appointments and therapies, but it's still time. We never wanted to spend that time where we did, it was necessary, though, and that's the moments you don't get to spend with your other children. Most children realize this and do not hold resentment, but it doesn't stop a parent's feeling of guilt. Logan's disability has opened so many doors for others like him in our area. Still, it also, in its way, forced us to spend time together as a family, not frivolous time like the time you spend in front of the television, but time with each other. We could have chosen a much easier path to follow. However, by allowing God's plan to work, our family has seen some truly remarkable things develop in our community. Regarding one another as more important than yourself is difficult, but in the end, the greatest reward.

CHAPTER 18

JUST GETTING STARTED

"You are never too old to set another
goal or to dream a new dream."

~ C. S. Lewis

The DREAMS Foundation of Acadiana is now running strong within our community. It's hard to believe that my wife and I scrambled to find something available for our son to participate in like a typical child just a little over thirteen years ago. It wasn't his choice to be born into a world asking him to face the obstacles he did. It wasn't our choice to raise a child with so many difficulties paving their future path. It was an unforeseen gift that showed us what the world was missing; a world focused on the ordinary. Our society is so focused on everyday life. We seem to concentrate on making life simpler and more efficient. Those that are different seem to be an afterthought. Our son just wanted to be like everyone else; he wanted the same things as children his same age had, and that shouldn't be too much to ask. His desire opened our eyes, not to just his aspirations, but others like him.

One of my favorite scripture passages of the bible is in the gospel of Mark 10:14 – 15, "Let the little children come to me; do not stop them; for it is to such as these that the kingdom of God belongs. Truly I tell you, whoever does not receive the kingdom of God as a little child will never enter it." Jesus points out that they should look through the children's eyes, look at their belief, faith, and love of God. That's what it's like in heaven. Jesus never said bring only the athletic blue-eyed males to me, nor did he say only take the prettiest of girls; he said, "Let the little children come to me; do not stop them." Why didn't he single them out, only asking for the best of the best? Because we are all made in the image of God. We assume God's image is what we consider God's image to be, not what the image of God is. We have been conditioned through paintings and artists' representations to picture God in a certain way. You will never see a portrait of God in a wheelchair, with Downs Syndrome features, or with any other disabling condition. Our picture of God is complete perfection in our minds, which does not involve blemishes of any type. Why, then does Jesus say, "Let the little children come to me; do not stop them." Why doesn't he specify which children? Because we are ALL made in God's image! This passage is clearly to remind us not only to look through a child's eyes, but all children are the image of God, and we must look at them with nothing but love.

Love has always been our driving force since we began creating and developing programs for children with disabilities in our area. It's so much easier to continue and work a little harder each day when you hear those words whispered into your ear, "Let the little children come to me; do not stop them." Our exhaustion, our desires, and our other problems in life can not get in the way of our calling; if we allow that to happen, we stop. I've always believed that the day my son asked me, "When do I get to play?" That question meant more than his desires; it was God opening our eyes to a bigger picture. It was a question all children with disabilities were asking, and sadly up and to that point, they were being turned away much like in Mark's passage.

Thirteen years into this and we've successfully opened, run, and or promoted nineteen-year-round sports and activity programs for individuals with special needs in our community. We service over 400 families around the area, some of which drive over seventy miles each week just to be involved What began with only the two of us has now blossomed into a substantial volunteer base of parents, friends, and family members wanting to help and continue to expand the opportunities for this population.

A few years ago, my wife contacted the Tim Tebow foundation about hosting his "Night to Shine" prom. Over the past four years, we've worked closely with area churches to make this prom happen. The night allows 150 individuals with special needs to experience prom as a king or queen that evening. It takes a small army of volunteers to put this prom together. Those volunteers need to be familiar with our kids. We just so happen to have that army now.

Eventually, we began to see friendships and bonds develop with our kids and our parents. We finally had a community who understood the things we all were going through; they understood how life was different for raising children with disabilities. Friendships help in so many ways, but there is always the need to do more. Recently my wife began a mother's support group meeting monthly to discuss specific topics that only moms can experience. The support group has about ten ladies to this point who share ideas, concerns, and a laugh or two. From speaking to several moms, I've discovered how therapeutic this group has been for them and now plan to begin the same group for our dads. One of the concerns found through the mother's group was the feeling of acceptance with our children in the church. Every church is different. While they express that they want to include our children, most do not possess the knowledge and resources to make this happen, leaving many of our families feeling left out. Because of this problem, we recently created a small faith group with our kids. The mom's present lessons about God in a simple way to help our kids understand the message, along with lots of singing, and of course, prayer.

Our children eventually become older, and their desires begin to change. We've always known they needed a sense of community; they needed to belong to something; that's why we developed and promoted year-round sports and activity programs. Now that they were becoming adults, they needed something more. They needed a sense of purpose, which led us to create the DREAMS Manufacturing company, allowing twenty-one individuals with disabilities the opportunity to work. No, it's not glamorous work, but it is a job. Listening to the employee's excitement about getting a paycheck or telling someone about their job shows the significance in their lives. Our biggest problem we've encountered since creating the manufacturing company is the limit we have on hiring. As we grow, we will provide more jobs, but growth takes time with any business. Several companies around the area have begun to notice our kids, which may eventually open doors into employment through their establishments. We are now seeing others in our community inspired to create businesses that will provide jobs for people with disabilities helping to fulfill that sense of purpose.

Recently, we partnered with the young man who has developed Unique fitness, a fitness program for our population. His business is booming. He needed his own space, so we have just leased a 2800 square foot facility that will house Unique fitness on one side and connected space for the Dreams foundation. Our goal with the new area is to establish a training facility to teach special needs individuals job-related skills. Building job skills are desperately needed to make them more employable. We will also use the space for some of our existing and newly developed programs.

We have offered and run a summer camp for the past five years for our population, from children as young as age five to adults with no age limit. While the summer camp began with only a few, we watched it grow to over 130 campers each year. Each camper experiences dance, art, fitness, science, magic, and many more activities throughout the week. The added plus that we have found is that many of our younger volunteers have moved on to college to pursue careers involving disability.

It has undoubtedly been a whirlwind of excitement and no not much rest in between programs. Still, the smiles and laughter we see at each activity supply that extra push we need to continue and look for more. Placing our trust and faith in God, we have seen why he selected us for this path. We've learned that no idea is too big or too small over the years, and with God's help, we can make it happen. We must rely on faith in many of our new programs as some seem to take longer to put together than others. One of those is our long-range project, our community. There are two primary concerns among parents when their child with special needs begins to get older. The first we have already tackled is their sense of purpose. We need that reason to get out of bed in the morning; look at someone and say, "Hey, this is my job; this is what I do!" The second concern is not that easy. That concern is the fear of the future for parents. What happens to our child with special needs when we pass away? In typical families, that question is still there. Still, the concern is not as great since typical children can gain further education and eventually achieve employment. The provided for eventually become providers, and the circle of life continues.

Unfortunately, this is not the case in many special needs families. Several individuals with special needs may never be able to take care of themselves without help properly. What happens to them? Does this burden pass to other family members? Are those family members willing to take on that responsibility? It's a lot to ask someone. Individuals with special needs have limited options. One of my biggest fears for my son is that my wife and I pass away, forcing Logan to live in a nursing home or a government group home. I can't begin to imagine how miserable he would be in either of those environments. If we asked his siblings, they would take care of him, but I don't want to place them with that responsibility. So, what is the answer? Our answer is in our long-range plans, developing a community for individuals with disabilities. A community where help is right around the corner twenty-four hours a day and seven days a week. A place surrounded by employers willing to provide work for our population. A place where obstacles of travel that many of our kid's face is taken out of the equation, as everything is easily accessible. A place where the Dreams foundation can continue to grow and offer year-round activities for personal enjoyment.

Is this possible? I firmly believe it is, but it will take years of work to make it happen. We're not talking about separating the disabled from the abled-bodied population at all; inclusive environments are critical. The community's creation would focus on our disabled population first, reversing what we see in typical neighborhoods. We know this isn't something that every individual with special needs will become a part of, just as not everyone participates in every program we offer. The idea is for those needing or wanting this type of neighborhood, the opportunity and choice if it's right for them. God has led us this far, and my wife and I believe we still have a long path ahead of us. The book of Proverbs 3:5 – 6 states, "Trust in the Lord with all your heart, and do not rely on your own insight. In all your ways, acknowledge him, and he will make straight your paths." Our path may be lengthy, and our complete understanding of how this can become a possibility is unclear. We still know that we have always put complete trust in God. I have no doubt this is his plan, and I have no doubt we will see it happen.

CHAPTER 19

AMAZING GRACE

"Be the change you wish to see in the world."

~ Mahatma Gandhi

Over the years, my wife and I have faced several obstacles on our path. It would have been easy to go the other way and chose a different direction at various points in our lives, but easy does not always mean better. We've argued and complained to each other, especially early on in our marriage, how this just wasn't fair. Why were we chosen to lead this life? Why couldn't our life be like everyone else, just ordinary? I think what helped us in those early years was realizing that typical is just plain dull. Yes, we had to do a lot more than your average family, and it was stressful. Still, when things became overwhelming for us, God would give us a simple reminder that we didn't have it so bad.

I'll never forget attending a parents' night out group put on by a local organization just a short time after Logan was born. The purpose was to introduce parents with disabled children to each other to discuss their feelings. We were seated across from a young lady, whom we began a discussion by telling her the details of what we had endured. She empathetically nodded as we talked and then told us about her situation. Her husband had left her after giving birth to twins. The twins were born with cerebral palsy, both non-verbal, both children needing wheelchairs for mobility, both needing feeding tubes to eat.

She was doing this alone! Bad became worse as she explained that she had an older son with the same complications and that her only help was her mother. The parent's night out was her first night away from her children in almost a year. I've never felt so small in my life; I wanted to crawl under the table, embarrassed that we had started our conversation with her with how bad we had it. My wife and I have never looked at our struggle as something significant since that evening, and I haven't missed a day in which I prayed for that lady and her three children.

We learned early on to put complete trust in God and our marriage. It was apparent we were given our situation for a reason. There is nothing special about us. We were just two people who fell in love, given a path in life completely unexpected, a road that many would have chosen to give up on and go the other way. When you place your trust in God, you first must realize it's not going to be easy. Through tough love, he teaches us, making us more capable with every step, wiser with every accomplishment. Arguing, complaining, and feelings of anger and depression do not cease. Still, you make it through those rough times, knowing you can face them again if needed. In the gospel of Matthew 16:24 – 25, Jesus tells us, "If any want to become my followers, let them deny themselves and take up their cross and follow me. For those who want to save their life will lose it, and those who lose their life for my sake will find it." My purpose in life is to help my wife and children get to heaven, and this passage gives me directions on how to do this. By denying ourselves of that everyday life we so longed for early on, we chose to take up this cross and follow the path given to us by Jesus. Most dads out there know after the late-night Christmas eve scramble to put the toys together for your children's excitement on Christmas morning. If you don't follow the directions, you're probably going to put it together wrong and cause yourself more work and frustration. So, it's always been uncomplicated for us just to follow the directions.

Watching the growth of our foundation over the years has been a true blessing. Finding an answer to Logan's original question opened our eyes to the bigger picture. We've never done anything for money or accolades; that's not what it was about; it was about the kids. It doesn't take long to fall in love with these kids when you begin working with them. Their joy lights up the room. I honestly see and hear Jesus through their laughter and smiles. Those are the simple rewards that give us the drive to continue. The gratitude of so many families has been humbling over the years. Neither of us asks for thanks for what we do; we only desire to make life better for these families. These are again small gifts that God gives us, letting us know we are accomplishing the task he has put in front of us.

Much of our devoted time has always been to the foundation and Logan's needs. We made sure to spend that one on one time with each of our kids. However, we've also encouraged their involvement in everything we were doing with the foundation, especially the activities. We always felt it was important for our kids to see and work with others like Logan. You never know how meaningful those life lessons can be from just a moment or two of interaction. We had to remind ourselves that God didn't just choose us to follow this path, but Monique and Lucas were also on this road, at least for a short time. They both always jumped in to help and never complained, quickly becoming part of our regular family time. It repeatedly shocked me at how my other two kids naturally assimilated into our programs as well as they did. They experienced firsthand some of what each of our kids and parents goes through. They learned how to work with each disability. Most importantly, they had fun.

Since becoming a special needs teacher, I've always said that I have the best job on the planet! I know this is what God intended me to do; I know this where I belong. I physically wake up each morning excited to go to work, excited to see my students, and to see what obstacles we can overcome that day. My wife can see it, my family sees it, anyone who knows me can see it, I'm going to work at a place that I love, and with kids I love. I know that my students will tell me they love me and mean it at least fifty times each day. I know that they will ask to hug me at least twenty-five times each day. That feeling has always confirmed that God was speaking directly to me many years ago; it was his design for me to teach kids with special needs, it was his plan, and I listened! My reward is knowing that he gave me this unique blessing that I get to receive every day I go to work. I get to develop personal relationships with these individuals and their families. Hopefully, I can help make this world a little better for them. Did I mention that I have the best job on the planet?

I take my job very seriously and continuously look for ways to better myself as a teacher for my kids. That's another blessing God gave me a few years ago when he led me to St. Thomas More Catholic high school, a private school with a mild/moderate program. Monique graduated from this high school in 2010, and my wife and I were impressed with the school and faculty. The school's focus on their patron saint's words, "God's servant first," can be seen and felt throughout the school daily. It just made sense to join their program. St. Thomas More Catholic high school gave me something that public schools couldn't, and that was they were genuinely behind our program and our work with our students. The support and love we receive each day from the faculty, staff, and student body are unbelievable. That makes an enormous difference in our students' growth and development, another daily reminder of God's intentions. The only thing is when things are going fantastic in all areas of my life, and I tend to see the red flags. I begin to anticipate something big coming, and big things can be terrifying.

The day before my fiftieth birthday, we were ending our regular Thursday mass with the entire school. We usually have school announcements after mass, but there weren't many going into the Thanksgiving holidays. That day was a little different as there was one extra-special announcement for many of our faculty members. In Lafayette, we have an organization that decided teachers needed recognition for their hard work and dedication. This organization is called the Lafayette Education Foundation. Each school year, they ask students, faculty, staff, and family members to send in written nominations of teachers, either past or present, that have impacted them. It's a huge honor to receive a nomination. The nomination means someone has been affected by what you do and took their time to write a nomination on your behalf. Here was the next big thing, I was one of 1,085 teachers nominated for teacher of the year! How amazing was that? Just the thought that someone out there took the time to write something about me was overwhelming enough. I remember feeling thrilled with pride and couldn't wait to tell my wife the news; what an excellent recognition.

Little did I know, this was only the beginning! A few weeks later, on December 5th, 2019, we were busy helping our students to prepare for the Christmas break. Our preparation takes a lot of planning and work. We must assemble presents for parents, faculty members, and staff that our students want to deliver. This year we decided to mix ingredients for cookies and place those into jars with baking instructions. Sounds simple, right!? We worked on this project with our kids in my room for a little over an hour. I turned to see our principal pop her head in to ask how it was going. Within seconds and before I could say a word, the rush of noise entering my room was breathtaking. I looked up to see approximately twenty-five people enter my room. They were throwing confetti, banging drums, shouting through megaphones, cheering, and setting off several other noisemakers. I had no idea what was happening; all I knew was both my arms were covered in brown sugar and some other sticky substance. These people needed to keep it down; they were going to disturb our math department. I went into full-on teacher mode to attempt a stop to this charade when I suddenly glanced down and saw a large banner with my name on it. I froze in my tracks; this was the selection committee for LEF! I had been named as one of sixteen finalists out of almost 1100 teachers nominated! No way this couldn't be real, could it?

To fully understand my shock, I must put the nomination process into perspective. Most teachers teach a larger number of students each year than what we work with in special education. Meaning there should be a more considerable amount of nominations for regular education teachers based on those numbers. Most of my students cannot sit down and write a letter of nomination, so this means they would require help from another source to do this. There are almost 2,600 teachers within Lafayette parish, all of who perform incredible tasks each day for their students. To be selected as a finalist meant that I had received an unimaginable letter of nomination. What an utterly humbling moment.

You don't find out who nominated you until the night of the finals in January. Almost three months from the time you received your nomination notice, so you now are left to wonder not only who but what could they have said about me? I'm nothing special; I just love my job. The local newspaper dropped by to interview me, and various faculty members congratulated me throughout the day. I don't think I stopped shaking with excitement; best of all, my typical hug count tripled.

Over the next two months, I received celebrity treatment, giving several interviews through the paper, local news channels, and of course, our school news program. Everywhere I went, people, I had never met before stopped me to congratulate me. LEF even furnished a complimentary tuxedo for the night of the finals. I'm just not one who likes the spotlight, but I must admit that the entire experience was thoroughly memorable.

The night of the final's ceremony arrived, and my wife and I, dressed to the nines. We were soon whisked away by limo to a pre-celebration with the other finalists and their spouses. I was a little nervous, but meeting the other finalists seemed to calm me down. Our teachers do some fantastic things in our community; these people were well-deserved nominees. We were grouped and taken to the ceremony by limo about an hour after the pre-celebration had begun. Upon arrival at the performing arts center, we received the full red carpet treatment. Excitement filled the air, complete with screaming fans, paparazzi cameras flashing all around, and local news crews attempting to pull you to the side for a quick interview. I felt like I was walking into the Academy Awards; it was unbelievable. I had to choke back some tears as I saw one of my students upfront waving and cheering me on; my emotions were in overdrive. My wife and I were finally seated, and the ceremony was beginning; she leaned into my side and asked, "Did you prepare something to say if you win?" I know I must have turned white as a ghost because to this point, that had never been a consideration, so I quickly answered back, "I won't win, I'm not going to worry about that." That was the first time I began to worry that I might win; the anxiety quickly followed.

The end of the evening finally came, and the other three finalists in my category and I made our way up on the stage. They were thrusting me into a situation where I was way out of my comfort zone for someone who doesn't like being in the spotlight. The lights saved me as I could not see anything past the front row, which would have launched me into a panic, seeing the hundreds of faces watching the ceremony. I prayed to God and asked that if he had chosen me to receive this award, please give me the words I would need to accept. My knees were shaking as they announced my name as the winner of the 2020 inspirational teacher of the year! I turned to see one of my students dressed up and walking over to present me with the award. I remember tears rolling down my cheeks as I walked over to deliver a few brief words. God gave me the speech I needed because I sure did not have anything myself; I was utterly overwhelmed. I was just a special education teacher, nothing in my mind as inspirational; I was just me. I loved my students, my job, my chosen path in life. To be recognized like this was never something I expected. I just enjoyed my profession and my students and only wanted to do the best possible job for them daily. I could feel God hugging me as I won; this had been his plan all along. I could hear him whispering in my ear; I told you this is what I intended you to do, and I felt just for a moment that this was a small slice of how Heaven must feel. Awards had never been important to me, but this was different; this was an amazing grace given to me to show me the why.

After the ceremony had concluded, we met in an after-party room, where I quickly learned who had nominated me. Our school librarian had submitted the nomination, but it wasn't just her nomination; she based it upon her interviews with my students. I still choke up when I think about that. Not only did she take the time to write the letter on my behalf, but she also took time to speak to each of my students and get their thoughts on nominating me. I can never thank her enough for doing this as it will always remind me that what I do is significant, what my wife and I do is important.

God has never made it easy for us, and we could have walked away at any time and chosen a much less complicated path to follow. He would have still loved us no matter what we decided. God presented us with a challenging route to follow, one that we accepted. Why do we do it? Jesus gives us the two greatest commandments in the gospel of Matthew 22:37 – 39, where he says, "You shall love the Lord your God with all your heart, and with all your soul, and with all your mind. This is the greatest and first commandment. And a second is like it; you shall love your neighbor as yourself." If you love someone and I mean genuinely love someone, you'll do anything you can for them. Through doing what he asked of us and loving our neighbor, we have seen firsthand how simple acts can change people's lives. Our foundation's growth is nothing more than a testament to what can happen when you follow God's plan. Yes, there will be pain and suffering, but this is true in all human life. The difference is that if you listen to God and follow his plan for you, you learn to deal with that pain and suffer differently. You understand how to turn it into love.

ABOUT THE AUTHOR

Brian Watkins is married with three children in Lafayette, LA. They became guardians to his wife's youngest sister after losing both of her parents at a young age. The couple's first son was born with a disability known as Spina Bifida. Brian is a special education teacher and holds a MA in special education. He and his wife developed the Dreams Foundation of Acadiana to provide programs and activities for individuals with special needs in their community. Brian and his family received the Governor's Gold Award as Family of the Year in 2009 for their work with disabilities within Louisiana. Brian also received the Governor's Gold Award as Educator of the Year in 2014 for his special education work. Most recently, Brian received the 2020 LEF award for Inspirational teacher of the year.

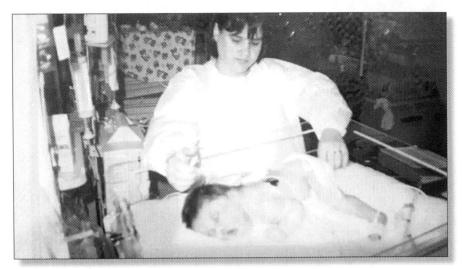

LOGAN IN THE NEONATAL INTENSIVE CARE UNIT
ONLY A FEW DAYS AFTER BIRTH.

LOGAN AND I EXCITED FOR OUR 1ST CUB SCOUT MEETING.

Logan and Lucas, both playing soccer on their own teams.

Logan swinging for the fences at the
Little League World Series 2011

OUR FAMILY AT LOGAN'S GRADUATION FROM HIGH SCHOOL.

DREAMS MANUFACTURING COMPANY – EMPLOYING
21 INDIVIDUALS WITH DISABILITIES.

BRIAN AND HIS STUDENTS BEING RECOGNIZED AFTER RECEIVING
THE LEF 2020 INSPIRATIONAL TEACHER OF THE YEAR AWARD.

OUR FAMILY AFTER I WAS ANNOUNCED THE LEF 2020
INSPIRATIONAL TEACHER OF THE YEAR.

My youngest son Lucas. Spending time with just each other.

MONIQUE OUR OLDEST, THE DAY OF HER WEDDING.

DREAMS FOUNDATION OF ACADIANA LOGO

Printed in the United States
by Baker & Taylor Publisher Services